Twerkin And The City

Ayana Ellis

Published by Purpose Publishing est 77, 2024.

TWERKIN AND THE CITY

First edition. March 31, 2024.

Copyright © 2024 Ayana Ellis.

ISBN: 979-8224203987

Written by Ayana Ellis.

2

Before we go any further, I think it is imperative that I preface this book with a disclaimer. I want to be crystal clear that this is not a book about *"how to get a man" "what needs to be done to snag a baller"* or anything having to do with pleasing or getting anything from the opposite sex. This book is less focused on how to get and keep men and more focused on how to keep ourselves in check! Throughout this book I share with you all the times that I fell short of what I say I'm all about and what I've learned in the process. We design our future, and we deserve the very best that this life has to offer us. We are life carriers and givers, and we deserve some damn respect! You should also know that I wrote this book because dating nowadays sucks and we need to discuss this as a family. So grab a glass of wine, curl up or put your earbuds in, and enjoy the journey of an unapologetic, mistake making, always-having-the-courage-to trust love one more time, woman by the name of Yaya.

ii

Before I tell you how I ended up getting all up in my feelings in Brooklyn one night, I want to tell you about what kind of friends I have. We give one another unfiltered advice. We hold each other down no matter what, we are honest with one another, and we push each other to be great. I'm the single girl in the group. Yes, all my friends are married. I never feel awkward around my married friends, ever because their husbands are good men and they too have become my brothers and want to see me happily married. I kept wondering why my beautiful black magical self was single, and one night in Brooklyn I got the answer. Before we get to the juicy stuff, this is the short story that led me to write this booklet, and why I chose this title, so that you can understand where I'm coming from.

Okay, so boom. My good, good girlfriend and her husband flew up from Atlanta to visit her brother in Bed Stuy, Brooklyn. I, of course, went to visit my friends while they were in town. We had a nice, elegant dinner around his lovely dining room table. I had to mention his lovely dining room table because number one, it was so lovely that it needed to be mentioned and two this is where the action took place. He pulled out some fancy ass glasses and to his dismay his sister, *my friend*, wanted to drink some real low-level libations. We scoffed at her as we were not here for her nonsense that day. Nobody was in the mood to nurse a baby headache all night because she wanted us to drink some liquid crack. Her brother pulled out the fancy bourbon glasses, and we rejoiced while simultaneously eating some delicious grilled food off his state-of-the-art grill and all was right with the world; it was a grand time. There was jazz playing in the background and what not, just a real stone-cold adult groove. My friends' daughter showed us a dance routine *of course* because what's a black gathering without someone's child showing us what they can do while we pretend to care so the adults can hurry up and get back to getting drunk while popping shit amongst ourselves. Her dance was cute though, all jokes aside. She choreographed the piece in memory of her grandmother. I believe Mother's Day was soon approaching, and she was going to showcase the dance at school. It was sweet.

As the evening progressed, our cups continued to runneth over, and laughter was ever present. Our plates filled with healthy delights, arugula and pumpkin salad, grilled meats with a special sauce made the night nice. It was a really nice day, and I got comfortable enough to start talking shit after bourbon refill number... probably 4, I don't know. I discussed my lack of patience for *everything* in life these days. At this age, I say don't argue with me. Women over 35 like me just don't have the bandwidth to deal with folks and their nonsense, mix that with me being a tactless Sagittarius, smother it with the fact that I'm the product of two Jamaican parents raised in some Brooklyn projects, and you got a cluster fuck of bumbaclotted, dead ass realness.

The older I get the ornerier I become because at some point you must be honest with yourself. I realized that I suffer from lackadickaphobia *often* by choice. I'm at my peak and can't get consistent sex because I am a single woman, and I don't want to be out there outsourcing my pu**y. I'm not cut out to be a hoe. I'm sort of like hoe adjacent, you know? I act up, then I back up. I'm not about that life 100%, and I'm all out of being in those dreadful situationships. I rather be alone before I waste my time playing with someone that I know isn't right for me. I want more than sex. I want more than a situationship. I want to have disgusting, filthy, vile, guttersnipe, straight-out-the-hood sex with the man I love and who loves me, wants only me, and respects me. Someone who belongs to me and is committed to me. I want a sure thing and being with just anybody just won't do. One of the main reasons most women even want to be in a relationship is to have consistent sexual relations, right? Just me? *Oh.* So, back to the brother's house in Bed Stuy. Here I was, as always, the inadvertent 3rd wheel because her brother is married as well. Hell everyone in my life is married, even my man.

JOKES! Relax, first wives club...

As my good-good girlfriends' husband "E" is talking, I thought back to when I went to Essence Fest 2019 with my other good-good girlfriend and her friends and they were telling me how men were looking at me, but I wasn't paying them any attention! They said things to me like:

"You just be looking straight ahead, you're not smiling, blinking, or looking at anyone!"

*"Ayana, these men are looking at you, and you have the "ni**a please look all on your face!"*

"Ayana you do not look approachable at all."

Me: *"But I am approachable and funny and nice!"*

Them: "*Yes we know that you are all of those things, you're a wonderful woman but how will a man know if you give off such a don't fucking talk to me, vibe?*"

Now, they have me thinking like damn, do I come off this way? Is it my fault that I'm single? Sometimes, I just have so much on my mind that I wear it on my face, *obviously,* but it is not a reflection of who I am as a woman. I'm very communicative, talkative, and approachable. I think I'm a good catch. I'm attractive, always ambitious, I never smoked crack, and I was not a prostitute in another town. I have one kid, no crazy exes, I take care of myself, I'm kinda funny, I'm cool as hell, my ass is real...major key, *and* I throw down in the kitchen. Okay, not throw down throw down, but a girl can burn. So, as I think about all the things that was said to me at Essence out of pure love, I now go back and forth for a while with E, discussing my standards, my needs, my wants and what I deserve. We talk about my shortcomings and my flaws as well, and of course I have none. Look, I am a perfect sweetie outside of this lazy eye. It's not me, it's them! But then E said the most profound thing that put it all into perspective. He said, "you know what it is, Ayana?" And as soon as he said that I knew that he had the answer. A man's perspective is always welcome because sometimes your girlfriends simply don't know what they be talking about. So when he said, "*You know what it is, Ayana?*" I eagerly pulled my chair up, sipped my drink, waited with bated breath, my hands folded, anticipating the gem I needed that would finally catapult me into the eternal love I deserve and desire. He told me where I was going wrong. His advice to me was real and simple... He said Yaya, "*You twerkin for the wrong ni**as.*"

"TWERKIN' AND THE CITY"

By Ayana Ellis

His wife and I laughed so hard when he said that. But he was telling the truth. Sidebar: Twerking for the wrong ni**as herein as referred to as "enword" shall I choose to call him such. Enword is not limited to one ethnicity, but to the entire male species. But what E meant by this was that I had given too much to the wrong men, and he was right. I have over the years. We all have. Come on sis don't do that, you gave too much to someone before, and you're probably doing it right now! I joked with him and said I'd write a book titled twerking for the wrong enword one day, and now here I am. I knew it would take some strength and humor to recount my dating experiences as a conduit into my advice giving. It's not easy "going back." But a friend of mine has a non-profit organization, and her tagline reads "Testimony Requires Transparency" and I couldn't agree more. It will take transparency to push through this. I must keep it real with myself first, which is sometimes not an easy thing to do. Once you're transparent you become susceptible to so many opinions and harsh criticism. Lucky for you all, I could care less what anyone thinks or says about me, so let me spill some of *my* tea to you, so that we can get better acquainted, right? Because I know that there is something in here that at least one of you can relate to. So here goes.

1 TESTIMONY REQUIRES TRANSPARENCY

I have been in quite a few relationships and situationships in my day, each of them lasting years beyond what they should have, each of them built on faulty foundations and a need to be loved, each one of them built on and believed to be "real" because of the trauma that it was connected to. In hindsight, I realized that I attracted men who fell in love with my pain and *need* to be loved, that I thought I hid well beneath my tomboy swag and "real" personality. I know my lowkey neediness as a *younger woman* made these men feel powerful over me. I mean who doesn't love a damsel in distress, right? They knew I had a need that they couldn't fulfill, but they pretended very well that they could, and I fell for it because I didn't know what support, love and a man having my back looked or felt like. So as a result, these men in my past got the best of me. I foolishly loved them how I wanted to be loved and not how they deserved. I learned a hard lesson which was to never treat a person how you want them to treat you, treat them how they deserve to be treated. None of those relationships were healthy, no matter how hard I tried to convince myself otherwise. But when you don't have any examples of what a healthy relationship is supposed to look like or what they should entail, you make the best of what you have, and you go with what you think you know. I made so many mistakes as it pertains to relationships. I've done a whole lot of taking on what I didn't deserve. But no matter what, I fought to not become bitter like so many women I've seen fall victim to their emotions and circumstances. If nothing else, I fought to keep some love inside of me because at the end of the day, love is strength, love is joy, love is abundance, love is me. I couldn't let some outsiders take my ability to love *and be* loved away from me by their cowardice actions. I tend to forgive everyone who has wronged me because it's the healthy thing to do. Forget forgiving because it's right. I forgive for the benefit of my soul, but it's still fuck you...with love. I refuse to carry someone else's load. Someone who was hurting, so they hurt me. When you forgive, you return the energy back to them and release yourself of all fuck shit.

At the tender age of 17, I was sentenced to an abusive relationship for 4 years of my life. I won't get into it, the details were already chronicled in my 2nd book Full Circle (2010). But the violence varied between physical, verbal, sexual, mental, and emotional. I was released from that prison totally fucked up in the head at roughly 21 years old. I came home a battered, confused, broken woman. I, like many women, had no idea the lingering effect that being abused could have on you specifically if you do not get the help you need. Between Stockholm Syndrome, PTSD, and never receiving the right help, I was totally messed up in the head and heart. Imagine your first try at a relationship, and you wind up in a real life "What's Love Got to Do with It" situation. I struggled with some of my emotions and thoughts 'til this very day because of that relationship because I spent half the time hiding how this relationship affected me because to be honest, I felt as if the people around me wanted me to just *get over it*. To not appear like a "victim" I soldiered on *unhealed* to please the people around me who had no idea the levels of abuse I had gone through. I personally think that they don't believe some of the gory details of my past. As a result, I paused my healing process and let anger, pain, hurt, humiliation, and poison fester inside of me over time. You can only imagine the havoc I wreaked on everyone in my life throughout my healing process because of anger and resentment. But let's scale back to me fresh out of this abusive relationship, 9 months to be exact when I met someone and "fell in love". Imagine having the courage to trust and love someone once more after going through something so disturbing. Again, hindsight is 20/20 and since my previous relationship was a nightmare, it was quite possible this man I met wasn't that special, and anyone after that violent relationship would be considered a dream. But here I was, 21 at the time, still very young and "wet behind the ears" nowhere near healed from the trauma I had just gone through, meeting a guy 5 years my senior with experience, and by experience, I mean he was someone's father. I had never dated a man with a kid and wasn't sure if I needed to know a specific set of rules in doing so. All I knew was that he was handsome, fun, and loved spending money on me. Money, money, money, money. That was my thing, and I'll share with you in a few why cash ruled everything around me...and still does.

Within the first 4 months or so of us dating, he told me he didn't want us to be just a *fuck thing*. He persisted and said he wanted me to be his girl. I obliged. Why not? We spent days and nights together. I wouldn't even go home after work a lot of times because we were constantly painting the town red, having to book hotel rooms throughout the city most nights, and purchasing me outfits to wear to work in the morning because our spontaneity didn't allow for me to pack overnight clothes...ever. After 3 years of bliss, and tons of red flags, (*baby mama drama*), I gave birth to real love, I had a child with him, a pretty little brown Princess whom I call Ladybug. But, expecting to be met with joy about the announcement of my pregnancy, I was met with bittersweet reactions. Now, during many love making sessions, he begged me for a "*pretty little girl,*" like most men do when they're up in something good, and like most men do when they didn't really mean what they said during sex talk, when I told him I was pregnant, he instead walked out of my life. I quickly found out I was the side bitch to his so called "crazy baby mama." Girl! Can you imagine? What a blow to my soul. I guess *I did* need to be well versed on how to date a man with children back then! Someone would have then told me that I was a fool to believe he spent the night just to take his son to school or that *she was crazy* and he spent holidays with his kid that's why he didn't spend them with me. I knew nothing back then about side bitches and baby mamas nor did I ever think I'd be a side bitch or a baby mama to *any* man. I thought highly of myself even though my actions and what I accepted sometimes would make one question that. But when you're young and in love, can't nobody tell you nothing. I would have never thought that after being with someone for 3 years and having his baby that he would react like this. So now, here we are, ***Aint Shit Enwords-2, Ayana-0.*** That situation, without a shadow of a doubt, birthed my permanent side eye and lack of trust in men on a different level. Sure, I experienced the utmost betrayal as the man before him beat the dog shit out of me and violated me in every single way a man can violate a woman every chance he got, but this enword here, walked out of my life during a time when he was supposed to hold me down the most. I was pregnant with his child. I will never understand how cold-hearted a motherfucka has to be to do that, not to mention he had a whole entire family while I was out here thinking that he was my man, and I was his girl. He made a fool out of me, and I never really trusted men after seeing how they were capable of hiding whole families in plain sight as well as turning their backs on you. I subsequently began to attract men *with situations* and *unfinished business* throughout the rest of my dating career. It was like a domino effect. I dated men who I felt had no staying power, *street dudes* for the most part, because they normally were in and out of town. I didn't have to get too attached, eventually the relationship would end for one reason or another beyond both of our control, but in the meantime, I would be afforded a financially stress-free life. Trips to Western Union were frequent, and I wanted for nothing when they were in my presence. I just wanted a man to adore me and do for me while in my presence and whatever he did when he left didn't concern me because in my mind all men had 2 or 3 different lives. I was just one of them. From my young 7-year-old mind, the adoration part that I yearned for came from what I saw my father do for my mother. He was her husband, father of her 4 children, the love of her life, they came from Jamaica together, and built a life. Me being the youngest, I saw a man that did anything for my mother. She was a kept woman in my opinion. We were never broke or hungry, *at least we didn't feel or look like it.* He went all out for her, he was sweet to her, he was sweet to his children. I wanted that in the men I dated when I got older. That is the core memory etched in my mind about my parents' relationship. He danced with her in the kitchen, he danced with me and my sister, and he loved on my older brothers. He was so cool. My dad, may he rest in peace, was a good man to my mother, he adored her, and he was a good father to us when he was there. He was so handsome, funny, charming, fly, he knew how to cook, he knew how to treat a lady, he loved my mother and most importantly, he was a G. But he left her when I was 7. The high tides of the streets swept him too far out into the middle of the ocean. It was hard for him to come back. He was gone. He drowned in the streets. He passed away 5 years ago, and I am so glad that we made amends. I was able to heal most of my broken heart and truly forgive him way before Cancer took his life, but man oh man the many years in between were filled with me trying to understand him, what his state of mind was like when he left us behind, and how his absence caused me so much heartache. The fear and shock of that abandonment followed me most of my adult life. I'm not sure if any woman reading this grew up without a father and can relate to that *vacancy*-feeling. I spent a lifetime trying to fill that hole in my heart.

But some traits were passed on as I spent a great deal of my life dating my father and being a product of my environment. When I was 14 and a virgin, my very first boyfriend was a hustler. He always bought me things. So early on it was planted in my mind that I didn't have to give my body away for anything material. If the man/boy liked you, he would still treat you with respect and will give you things without you having to give up a thing. And I still believe that. At 17, my abuser lavished me with expensive things from Versace shades, butter leather pants, Cartier wrist wear, diamonds, you name it. Yes, it was the 90s. My daughter's father spared no expense when it came to making sure I had a good time and got what I wanted when he and I were together, so it kind of stuck with me from a young woman that men were supposed to spend money on their girl, woman, shorty, whatever. So as time went on, that's what I attracted, *men who spent.* I didn't know back then that a man spending money on you meant absolutely nothing if he wasn't investing in you. But that was my mentality as a young woman. I've grown leaps and bounds since then. But between back then and when I finally became a woman, *forreal,* it was a constant struggle between being honest about the love I *truly* wanted and being a billy badass to avoid getting hurt. My temper was ghetto red hot. That is how I spent my 20s, raging against the machine, raising a kid by myself, and thuggin my way through these enwords. I was hard, angry, mad, hurt, heartbroken, lost, void of fucks to give, and sometimes physically violent toward the men I dated. I was so very much unladylike. I remember dating a guy and showing up to his house with a black eye that my daughter's father gave me for not wanting to be with him. That was the end of him and I. How could I so nonchalantly bring all this toxicity to another situation? I had the nerve to be unbothered at that! But deep down I was a broken bird. I disguised it as *"No fucks to give."* I thought it made me a woman. I thought it would protect me from being treated like a sucker. Oh what a time to be alive! I was out there mad as hell like, *I'm puttin' cases on all you bitches! You think you can do this to me?*

By the time I turned 30, I left a plethora of dead bodies in my wake, and I don't mean dead bodies in the sense of how many men I slept with, I simply mean the energy I exuded amongst other things. The people I killed in my head and with my words, ok and yeah, and a few bodies too. I was no longer living in New York because the city was just unkind to me. I damn near got chased out of Brooklyn because of my bad decisions and the heckling that followed. Before I moved out of town, I had a "brief encounter" with a guy that owned a home downtown Brookly, not knowing that he resided in Atlanta where I was moving to in a matter of days. He made sure to look me up when I reached my destination. *Girl.* What a rollercoaster of unnecessary fuck shit that situationship entailed. But see, when you're hopeless, and you don't know what you want, you settle for any damn thing, right? I had not a care in the world, and he simply fed off my youthful barbaric behavior (*I was 14 years his junior*) and my "fuck ni**as, get money" attitude. He indeed provided both, *of course*. I'd have it no other way. You couldn't date Ayana without spending. As long as my daughter was eating, I was cool. My faith in men was in the trash so if nothing else, while I'm out here working hard, writing these books, and raising a child, you will contribute to the Ladybug Gotta Eat Fund. But then one day out of the blue, I began to mature. My daughter was around 3 years old or so and starting to point and talk shit, so I had to straighten up. I thought about her childhood. I didn't want her growing up seeing mommy unstable, so I had to start moving differently and figuring out a way to attract a better way of life. I was turning 30, I always kept a good job and always carried myself respectfully, but that wasn't enough. I had to upgrade my mentality. I wanted more out of life. I had no idea where to start because my mind held a barrage of bad experiences that overpowered the good ones, but I knew where I stood in that moment wasn't cuttin' it. He began wanting more of the woman I was slowly but surely becoming. But I couldn't see past the fuckery that he and I started off with. You see, we started off one way, and I never took him seriously nor did I think he would take me. We never wanted one another in a way that a man and woman should. It was all lust and fun Atlanta nights on both ends. We had what we had, it was what it was, and I had no desire to try to turn his hoe-ass into a house husband. He began to wear me down with his advances of wanting to take things further. He became more serious, more consistent, more involved in my life and my daughter's life. So, I finally considered giving in, not 100%, but a "let's see" kind of thing. I had no expectations and thanked God I didn't because the moment I got just a *little pink,* he decided he had something he wanted to share with me because he "didn't want to lie." *Sidebar: You know, you gotta love these honest enwords. But let me tell you how I feel about a man telling me the truth, trying to come off as honest, fuck you!* Have you ever had a ballsy ass man come at you with the *"yeah I got a girl and I just want to be upfront with you. I don't want to lie to you and play games."* Then, he proceeds to try to get at you? Right there, at that very moment, is the determining factor on whether he will respect you or not. Like, right at that moment, when he is done speaking and he takes that shallow breath and tries to keep a straight face in anticipation of your answer, praying that you are desperate enough to talk to him even though he has just told you that he is in a relationship, is a matter of pimp or die. Well cut my legs and call me shorty, this *honest motherfucker* informed me that the woman he *allegedly* broke up with was having his child. In fact, she was 6 months pregnant. How darling of him to break the news to me while we were out having dinner at Jermaine Dupri's restaurant Mother's Day weekend.

Aint shit enwords up 500 points, Ayana-0. I can tell you this, he was the end of an era. I was officially off my bullshit, done and ready to move on from this cycle of men that I was attracting. I was ready to start over with life period. I was done with the games.

So now here I was, mentally and emotionally drained for the God's, morally bankrupt, and just fed up. But I had to soldier on. I took some time to myself, and I realized I hadn't been alone since I began dating at 14. My first real relationship was bloody, violent, and anything but lovely. My relationship after that produced a child, and I was betrayed in the worst way. With many more events in between, it was trauma after trauma after trauma. Then I wound up out of town still dealing with fuck boy shenanigans. I needed a break from men, period. I occupied myself with raising my child, and my writing career, as I happened to complete 4 books at this point of my fuckboy marathon. It was the only thing that kept me sane. I wrote my way through *everything*. It was a full-time job to stay fuck boy free. So I packed up my things and moved to a wonderful town called the Wish a Ni**a Woods. Most, if not all, the people in that neighborhood got along and wished for the same things as well. The Wish A Ni**a Woods is a small, tight knit community where everyone is on the same page. But guess what happened, as I wished a ni**a would? A ni**a did!

Three months after that Mother's Day massacre and temporarily giving up on men, a man walked into my life and this relationship turned out to be the most beautiful and kindest relationship of them all. But I was toxic as hell inside from everything I had experienced up to this point. I was angry when I met him, outta pocket, and didn't care about anybody's feelings. Why should I have cared? Nobody cared about mine! For some odd reason during this season of my life, I wanted my father bad! I needed to talk to him, I needed some guidance. Though he lived in LA, we kept in touch, we talked, I loved him, I forgave him, we were building. But I didn't know where he was for a brief period in my adult life, he sort of fell off the map before resurfacing a few years later, so when I needed him most, *once again* he was not around. So every daddy issue I had was magnified, every heartbreak I ever experienced, every flaw and every hurt, I walked in it, and wore it on my sleeve. I suffered from abandonment issues. Here I was in this new town, with my small child, alone, just thuggin' it. Why was my life like this? Where the hell was my superman? He showed up in a Yankee fitted, True Religions, a fatigue army style shirt, and some fresh kicks reeking of some of the best marijuana life had to offer.

Instantly I thought, fuck boy, like I need another one of these. But within 48 hours, we bonded and connected in a way that I had never experienced before. It was some spiritual kind of thing I felt. I thought I may be bugging, so I didn't say anything. He would look into my eyes and just *listen* to my energy. He wouldn't say much, he wasn't a talker. He just observed me in a way that kind of hypnotized me. I never felt the urge to do him like I did the others, you know, that violent, lashing out, rah-rah shit. It was not happening with him. He shut me down without demanding a thing or opening his mouth. It was just a vibe that he would give me that told me I needed to chill. And so I did. His quiet confidence turned me on and made me straighten my back a little and walk a little taller. He was so hood, but he was equally solid. He carried himself differently than anyone I've dated. He carried himself with a sense of respect, and he made me feel safe. That was when I realized this was a feeling, I had to have no matter who I was with. A feeling of safety and comfort. So in a matter of time, I began to tell him my deepest, darkest most vulnerable thoughts, without being so violent about it, without making him feel as if it was his fault or his job to clean up someone else's mess. Instead of lashing out to get the attention I needed, I learned how to communicate. For the first time in my life, I actually communicated with the man I was dating, verbally and mentally versus violently, emotionally, or sexually. I grew as a woman because of how he allowed me to just be free. He became my best friend. Being with him made me realize what I wanted in a relationship because all along I had no idea what I wanted. Well yeah, I did think I knew what I wanted. Good sex, money, friendship, it was all so basic. The men before him hadn't touched me in a way to make me want more. With him, I started to think about having a family, stability, security, lifelong partnership, fellowship, understanding, respect, love, joy, peace, and a home because he made me feel protected and safe just by his energy alone, something no man had ever made me feel. I wanted to be my best for him. I enjoyed loving this man. He truly melted the ice around my heart by just being a genuine person and communicating with me in ways that showed me he cared for me outside of the bedroom. He had my best interest at heart and pushed me to be a better person, he tried his hardest to love me through my emotional complexity though. I wasn't easy to deal with. Even with all his imperfections, he loved me with all he had. He loved me, especial-ly different, he did. But he was the lessor of all evils because he too had some shit with him (*that's a whole 'nother book*) but his good more than outweighed his bad. Despite everything he had done for me to better me as a woman, be it my living and financial situations, my mental/emotional condition, and my all around being, you know; just having that effect on me that a good man will have on a woman sometimes. He did something that nobody ever cared about me deeply enough to do. He catered to the little girl in me that missed her father. He doted on that part of me. He dove *that deep* into my soul to get to the root of my behavior. He watched me, he studied me, he learned me and knew what to do and *not to do or say* without me mentioning a thing. It was then that I opened up and expressed to him the impact my father leaving had on me as well as my abusive relationship, my ex abandoning me during my pregnancy, and some experiences I had in the past. I never really got a chance to break down and cry about these things before meeting him. I'm in my 30s at this point, with all of this bottled-up pain I never really got to be honest with anyone about up until this moment. I was always hard, tough, strong. I had to poke my chest out and be a strong woman for myself, for my daughter, and for anybody who was watching me, praying on my downfall, leaning on me for strength, or looking up to me as a testimony. And now here I was, 7 years old again, in front of this grown man. He gave me a safe place to cry for as long and as hard and as often as I needed to. He gave me space to grow, to heal, to transition into whatever was to come. He babied and coddled me like a child but respected me as a woman if that makes sense. He didn't use it against me or throw it in my face. He didn't manipulate me or make me regret sharing any of my secrets with him. We never argued or fought. We talked out everything. We immediately apologized if some shit came out wrong. We didn't play games or hold grudges. We were straight up with one another. We hated to see one another upset. We had each other's backs. I hit the jackpot! I became codependent on this man's love because it indeed was the warmest, not to mention safest love I'd ever experienced and I did not, for a moment, want to live without it. I didn't know what it was like for a man to have your back, to hold you down, to be there for you without you having to throw hints or ask. And here he was, my security. He was my drug and my rehab. He was my safe place and keeper of all my secrets. And no matter how wild his life was, he made time to make sure I was okay. He did more than financially take care of me, he cared for me as a friend, a woman, a mother, a healing soul. He was a man of his word. Anything he said he would do for me he did. So when the feds snatched him out of my life without warning, after being with him for many years, you can only imagine how hard my high came crashing down. When he left, a huge chunk of my heart went along with him. I was done, at my wits end like Diana Ross in Lady Sings the Blues...baby put me in a strait jacket and kick me down a flight of stairs! I was done and did not know whether to shit or go blind at this point. Somebody broke into my home and stole every fucking thing but the kitchen sink. That's how I felt. I hit the floor. I was at rock bottom. What was I supposed to do without him? But one thing was for certain, as bad as losing him hurt, I knew I was loved, because he left me softer than I was before he came. I read that quote somewhere and thought of how perfect it described me. This relationship was a turning point for me. I couldn't go back to how cold hearted I once was. I was forever changed. I was now on a mission to duplicate this love I lost and that meant a whole lot more mistakes were to come as I chased this high. But one thing was for certain, this love taught me that real love existed, and it didn't have to come with pain before pleasure. It didn't have to be struggle love. The kisses didn't have to come after the punches. The I love you's didn't have to come as a result of guilt. The gifts didn't have to come after the infidelity. Love was possible without pain. There were good men out there and I was deserving of one.

But back to black I went as you could imagine, my heart physically broken, the aching pain in my chest just wouldn't go away. I lived in the dark and drank myself stupidly and up a few dress sizes for a long time until that second chance to breathe again arrived. You ever experience dark times and then out of the blue sky you wake up one morning and things are just different? I took advantage of the second wind and pulled myself up. A year had passed since I lost my love, and I was healing at a nice pace. A little bit of life crept back in me. But then during a Lasik surgery consultation, I was diagnosed with an eye disease called keratoconus that was slowly but surely deteriorating my eyesight in both eyes. I had double eye surgery within the same month and let me tell you, this was the most traumatic event I ever experienced to date. I fell back into a dark hole and during healing, I got fired because I wasn't healing fast enough. The steroids they prescribed had me out of whack. I was gaining weight and going through hell on the inside. During the entire time I spent in darkness, I never felt so lonely. Though my friends and family took such great care of me around the clock because I was visually impaired, that lonely feeling would not go away. I relapsed and began missing my ex. All I could think of was that he would be right here taking care of me. I cried every day and night for months, this aching feeling inside of me was consuming me. I prayed a lot and though I temporarily lost my sight, my vision couldn't have been clearer. I thought about getting old and sick and not having a partner to hold me down. These are things we don't really think about when choosing a mate. All these relationship related scenarios began to play in my mind when the only thing I could do at the time was think. I suffered from anxiety and realized how serious depression was and could get. I was never diagnosed, but I had the craziest thoughts, and my lows were *low*, my pain was so real, the black outs and the crying, the neglect of self and the mood swings, the zoning out and disconnect, *the alcoholism*. Most notable was when I used to wake up disappointed that I wasn't dead after drinking shit loads of vodka, using steroids, and popping painkillers. I didn't legit want to die, but I would wake up so damn tired like shit, it would be nice! I couldn't even muster up the energy to bathe. Then one morning, my homeboy Tone called to check on me and to see if I received the sun blocker shades he got me, because after the surgery my eyes have since been very sensitive to light; nonetheless, his comedic timing was perfect and was what got me out of bed on day 4 of not washing my ass.

Tone: Hey pretty lady how you feeling? Do you like the glasses I sent you?

*Me: *grumbly grouchy* thanks Tone yeah*

*Tone: Come on pretty lady, you sound so down, you are going to get better, trust and believe. (or something to that affect he said) Me: *rambles on about being so down and out, keeping my shades drawn, not eating, having to paint a smile on my face before my daughter came home from school because I didn't want to bring her down with me. Then I said Tone, I haven't even showered in like 4 days.*

Tone: WHAT? You mean to tell me you laying around the house fucking stink? Nah, get your ass up and wash your ass, you too fine to be stinkin', I'll come help you wash your ass, but wash your ass. Your ass is too big to go unwashed."

He tore into me so badly about lying in the dark for 4 days unbathed that I eventually got out of bed. I laughed my stankin' ass all the way to the bathroom. Thank you ToneBonePatron as I call him. Because anybody that battles depression knows it's real, you can go days without even thinking about bathing. It's not until your pets start nibbling on you because you smell like a carcass or your kid walks into your room and says *ma, you stink* that you need to do something about your situation. Yes, that actually happened. Meanwhile, my bills were backed up, Christmas was coming, and I had a whole daughter to provide for. It was so damn hard because I had lost my job, but there was no time to feel sorry for myself. I had to get up and do something about my life. I had a choice to make, and that choice was to grow up and glow up! I had to come out of that dark cloud that seemingly followed me everywhere. Fuck shit begets fuck shit. I was doing fuck shit, accepting fuck shit, and living fuck shittedly. I had no one to blame but myself. It was but for so long I could blame my absent father and the aint shit enwords around me. I had to look in the mirror and say Ayana, It's you! You are doing this to yourself! It was that simple. My life choices were a reflection of what I thought I deserved at the time. We all know you date at the level of your esteem, right? So if I'm out here dating aint shit ni**as, then guess what? I ain't shit either. That was a hard pill to swallow. It was time to think better of myself, think more highly of myself, and stop making excuses for any and everything going on in my life. I had to have a pep talk with my damn self: You are a grown woman now Ayana, cut the shit. You may not be responsible for what someone has done to you, but you are 100% responsible for your own healing.

So now, fast forward to how I began to heal *forreal*. I had to unlearn the old ways. I had to reprogram my mind. I was no longer in survival mode. I no longer looked to others to make me whole. I no longer needed to hold on to old thoughts and memories for comfort. It was time to create new and better memories. It was time to do things differently. "*When I was a child, I spoke as a child, I understood as a child, I thought as a child: but when I became a woman, I put away childish things.*" Ladies, there comes a time in your life when you have to dead everything and everyone and begin to focus on where you are trying to go and what your heart truly desires! You must get ahead of whatever your issues are. You must figure out a way to detach from anything and everyone that means you no good. You must fight for the life you want and deserve. Be better, do better, live better, think better, talk better. *Learn how to pray for better things!* You must stop telling yourself lies. Own your truth. Own what happened, own who you are, who they were, what you allowed. Own it! Then, release it! You will have no use for it or any reason good enough to hold on to anything or anyone that hurts you. Our beloved Toni Morrison said it best, "*You wanna fly? You gotta give up the shit that's weighing you down!*" I realized I would continue to fall into the same cycles of bullshit if I didn't hop off that hamster wheel and go a different way and forgive myself. I was tired of feeling forlorn, tired of feeling down. But when you aren't loving yourself right you leave the door wide open for folks to come in and mistreat you as well. I started to take self-inventory. *Ya, what are you filling yourself up with daily?* For sure, everything I was doing, thinking, speaking, living wasn't doing me any good, so I let go of it all. I had nothing to lose and everything to gain. I was very careful of who and what I listened to, what I watched on television, my music choices, what I put in my body. All of that had to be closely monitored. Lastly, the main and most important thing I did was get really honest with myself. Listen! That self-talk is some real, serious, crispy chicken business. You know the conversation I'm talking about; the one when you sit on the edge of your bed, you hang your head low, let those tears fall freely, and you start talking to yourself, praying out loud, forgiving yourself and promising yourself that you will never accept certain things again. When you start damn near begging God to please save you, please remove certain people, thoughts, and ways out of your life. When you start begging God to remove whatever love you have in your heart for a fuck boy, so you can move on. When you start pleading with the universe to please release you from all things negative and to please bring you some new energy, a new way, a new day. When you find yourself screaming, God please I'm so tired! You start convulsing asking God to strike you dead if you go against the grain. When those snot bubbles form and you start gagging on your own tears and choking, you know it's real, you know you have simply had enough of the bullshit.

By the power of Greyskull God, I wanted to be made over! I was done, I wanted more, better. I saw what God was doing for others and asked him to please do the same for me. I just wanted peace of mind more than anything. I wanted the lies I told myself to go away. I wanted to bury the memories. I wanted the past to stay there. I wanted to be made over! I wanted to stop running from myself. Every time I thought I had gotten away from dealing with my issues, there I was, showing up wherever I went. You cannot run from yourself. You will always meet yourself at each destination. I was tired of that. I wanted to be brand new. I envisioned the life I saw for myself and began to take steps toward it. I was no longer attached to the things I held on to. It was time to level up and get out of that dark ass place, that comfort zone, because wasn't nobody sending lifeboats for me. Let me tell you something, folks will stand around and watch you drown while recording your last breaths. Then they will cry, talking about they wish there was something they could have done to save you. I had to start telling myself the truth about me, and it was not easy. I cried, I was ashamed. It took me being alone, withdrawing from everyone and learning to love myself and enjoy myself before I could step back out and enjoy others. It took work, it took dedication, a dedication that nobody in this world will have for you to be great other than yourself! I know many of us hide our truths and as a result of that we inadvertently isolate ourselves and wind up feeling alone. We beat ourselves up for the mistakes we make along the way. We hold on to relationships, we hold on to memories, we go back and forth and waste so much time hoping things will change. Nothing will change unless we do. Some way, somehow, we have to find the will and the strength to pull ourselves up and get our heads above water, so we can survive and live another day. We all make mistakes, it's not just you, baby girl. Your friends and family fuck up too, some people are just really good at hiding their mistakes because they want to appear perfect. Don't be deceived. Every one of us fuck up from time to time or all the time.

But you have to learn to live with regret, and as bad as we just want to slip into eternal sleep because it's easier to give up, we cannot. We don't want to talk about our mental health because it's hard to even identify what we are feeling sometimes. We have people around us that will accuse us of *acting like victims,* and they put a time limit on when we should get over the trauma in our lives. Or they accuse us of overreacting and brush it off. This causes us to suppress our pain and put on a brave front like everything is okay. It's okay not to be okay. Don't let anybody speed up your healing, sis. Take your time and as long as you are making progress then to hell with what anyone says. Be patient with yourself, you are doing the very best that you can, dear.

The moral of the story is this:

Grow through what you go through.

2 SISTAS, HOW YAWL FEEL?

So, let's chat, how are you doing, lovebug? What is happening in that pretty little head of yours that keeps you from reaching your personal goals of happiness and inner peace? What's bothering you? Did you tell someone? Do you have someone you trust to share your heart with? I've talked to lots of women (*half of which live right in my damn head and the rest are women that I am surrounded by personally and social-medially*) and we all are scratching our heads trying to figure out what the hell keeps leading us down the yellow brick road to fuckboyville and depression. I find that so many of us are so depressed and filled with anxiety because of who we allow in our space and because we are not properly healing from what happened to us before we let them into our lives. Many of us are unhappy but life is too damn demanding to slow down, even if it's just to cry for a while. *We need to cry.* I heard someone say crying is like taking your soul to the laundromat, and I couldn't agree more. You must let out that good ole ugly cry occasionally. You know the cry. The one that results in a headache and a 5-hour midday nap. The one that pours from your soul, makes your nose run snot like a faucet, and gives you clearer vision when it's over. We can't keep beating our chests and subscribing to the notion of being superwoman to everyone but ourselves. A lot of us are **over**worked and ***under***loved. We bust our asses to get an education, so we can live a good life. We bust our asses to start businesses, to raise our children, to look good and feel good about ourselves in a world where we are bullied into hating ourselves for how we look physically, our hair texture, our complexion, what we wear, how we talk. It's always something for us to battle. After dealing with the world, we come home to ourselves, nobody there to love us, nobody to tap us on the ass and ask us how our day went, no one to root us on after we spent the whole day rooting for everyone else. Sometimes, you don't realize how lonely you are until you come home to yourself and have a moment alone without the grind, the kids, the hustle, the friends. It's okay to admit and embrace the fact that you are

lonely. *I think we usher in depression and anxiety when we hide what hurts us instead of trying to heal what hurts us.* A lot of women I have talked to haven't dealt with their "daddy" issues either. They just grew older and assumed that they were too old to still have these issues, so they suppressed them. A lot of women are working jobs that they hate, too afraid to step out on faith and let their talents shine. A lot of those same women don't have a good circle of support around them so now they're doubly depressed because their circle is wack and they're stuck in a cubicle. And it's not just "they" it's us. It's you. It's me. You are dealing with depression and loneliness because it's hard out here for a black woman doing the damn thing, but not being properly loved. *We need love.* A lot of women beat themselves up for not accomplishing or being where they thought they would be by this age. Is that woman you? It's no secret that women, *specifically black women,* need support and love more than any living thing on this planet; and so, we began creating sister circles and women's empowerment groups to love on one another because nobody seemed to care. Sad to say, most of those groups are just a bunch of mean girls in nice outfits, cliqued up to make other women feel unworthy...*at least that's what I heard.* So where do we go if we can't lean on one another? **THERAPY.** Please go see someone and talk about your problems, get unbiased advice, get better, sis because the world needs your testimony. Because when your mental state and emotions are all jacked up, the fuck boys creep in, seeping through the cracks of your current condition, lying dormant like a disease, waiting for the moment when you are on the up and up to flare up on your ass like herpes or hatch like a fucking foreign insect, infecting your entire person. Harsh, I know, *but real.* There's such a thing as energy suckers, and you have men and women alike who come around you to absorb everything good about you, your time, your advice, your joy, your *you*. Then they leave you with nothing because they have nothing to offer in return. You're so busy giving you don't even realize how much has

been taken from you until you're suffering from anxiety and depression, and nobody understands or can help you. Or they don't even realize what you're going through because you are the "strong" friend. You are so programmed to be strong and to keep things together you don't even give yourself a moment to feel the reality of what is going on around you. Stop for a second today and just cry if you need to. Being

vulnerable is one of the strongest things you can be! So don't feel as if you are weak for showing emotion. You can't keep all of that bottled up! That's probably why you have high blood pressure now! And try not to tell your friends in distress to "be strong" and that "it will be okay." If you don't have anything of substance to say, just don't say anything. It's okay to just listen. "Be Strong' and 'It will be okay' "comes off as dismissive and insensitive. Perhaps right now they want and *need* to feel weak and fall apart because sometimes falling down is the only way to get back up! Perhaps they need to cry and for one moment sit in the fact that it won't be alright, at least not right now, and be okay with that. Perhaps they don't need nor want the pressure of being strong. Maybe they want and need a moment of weakness. Allow them to be and do just that. Allow your loved ones the space and comfort of knowing they can cry, they can fall apart, they can hit the ground, and that's okay because you have their back, and you won't judge them. Most strong folks don't fall apart because they don't feel as if they have anyone there to help them pick up the pieces again the way they do for other people. It's the lack of security that (black) women have that forces us to endure and take on so much because who else will do it, right? Wrong! Fall apart if you must. Cry when you need to. Have your moments of weakness as much as you can. It doesn't mean that you are weak at all, it means the complete opposite. It's okay to admit the areas of your life where you feel weak. You cannot heal what you hide! Let go of anything or anyone that is weighing your mind and heart down. It's time to fly far away from these fuck boys (*and girls if they are taking advantage of you*)! Yes, this book is about self-love and twerking for the right enword. So fly so far away to where a fuck boy can't even see you! Mary J. Blige did not glow the fuck up after her divorce from broke ass, drunk face Kendu, get her body snatched, go on tour around the world with Nasir Olu Dara Jones' *foine* ass *and* spend $18.5 trillion dollars on riding boots this year alone, for you to continue letting enwords drag you through life! And before you step out into the world in search of or trying to attract your *him* or anything great into your life, you must fix you first. You must make sure that inside, you are stable, safe, secure, loved. It's time to go out there with your head and your standards high and get what you deserve! There is no need for you to remain in this dark, heartbroken, pitiful frame of mind. No more playing coy for the boy. No more playing small and humble. You are dope, you are worthy, you are wonderful, and you are everything someone out there is praying to find, but you gotta start dodging the raindrops, sis. Come on!

The moral of the story is this:

Until you have had enough, you will continue to suffer. Don't You Ever Want More?

3 FOOLISH

Phew~ so now that we got *that* part out of the way, let's take a journey, shall we? We moved on from *woe is me*, to brand new me. Yes, there is so much more work to do, but the load is a little bit lighter when you acknowledge your part in the bullshit. There is so much more to learn but thank God you're not where you used to be. You are now ready to level up because failure brings growth, and we aren't about to let what we've been through deter us from where we are destined to be, right? We will continue to fall 9 times and get up 10, period. I know for me, once I dumped that heavy ass load, I felt great and immediately started doing my spring cleaning. I religiously prayed and saged but could not for the life of me understand why I was so damn unsettled, *still*. My mind was always so heavy and consumed with a bunch of nothing, and it was driving me crazy! Have you ever felt so miserable, and you sat and thought about everything that was going on in your life? You do a G check like okay, what's good: I got a job—check, shelter—check, food—check, edges—check, my kids are okay—check, I got money left over after paying rent— double check, my car running decent—check, so what could be the issue? Well, I replayed that over and over in my head then had an aha! moment. I finally realized I was unsettled because I was still playing myself. Yup, I was holding on to something familiar instead of throwing it out. We tend to do that sometimes as we transition to a better way of life. Change is scary, so we play both sides until we are sure. But you gotta pick a side, baby girl. You are either going to stay in the sunken place or transition into a better way.

I realized I still harbored resentment and hurt over the things I experienced. I moved on by *suppressing* the traumas, not realizing that to be totally free I needed to be healed from it. So as a result, I found myself returning to it every once in a while, because it felt familiar. I was playing stupid ass games and winning stupid ass prizes. I was giving to, spending time with, thinking about or sexually active with individual(s) that were no good for my mind, body, or soul.

These people contributed nothing of value to my life and that is why I was so unsettled even after all the hard work I put in to be a better person. So I did some more work. I trained my mind to think of positive things whenever thoughts of the past tried to creep in. I started working out, I wrote another book, I found activities and things to do to occupy my mind. I poked my chest out and dealt with the backlash I would get from cutting people off and letting them go. I turned down invitations to be anywhere near anyone I used to deal with. I stayed out of their neighborhoods and away from mutual friends. I carved out an entirely new life for myself and slowly, but surely let go the right way. When the past called, I no longer answered to fulfill my ego. *Oh this enword is calling me, I know he misses me.* No he's calling you because he thinks you're stupid enough to pick up and give him the time of day. I stopped entertaining the circus clowns. The more I distanced myself from everything that was hindering me, the better I began to feel. If you do not know what is wrong with you, consider the fact that you too, maybe spending too much time *thinking* about someone who isn't thinking about you at all. Maybe you too are *wondering* about or *waiting* on someone who isn't reciprocating that same energy. You still might have some residual leftovers you need to return to sender. Give that energy back sis! You don't need it! Give it back. Stop taking the calls, he doesn't miss you, and he's testing your stupidity. Shake that shit off. Give it back to him, *to all of them,* to whoever is still on your shoulders, dust em off! Give that energy back. Stop having conversations about him, stop wondering, stop talking about who he was, be real about who he is, he lied to you sis, he's not a good dude, he ain't shit, he showed you, why won't you believe it? Stop it right now. Give it all back. Stop listening to negative, downtrodden, low vibrational conversations. Decline all invitations to pity parties and fake ass apologies. Stop giving him your time and your body. Stop twerking for this dude. He does not deserve it. You feel off key because you just might be *laying up* with someone who you do not feel connected to or loved by *after* he is done sweating out your silk press. It can't feel good to be mistreated after you paid damn near $1,000 for that Kinky, Brazilian, Water Wave, Body Bounce, Peruvian, Spanish Wavy, Indian, Straight Perm, 67inch unit to look good for some raggedy ass enword that didn't even contribute one dime to your hair, just to have him send you home looking like you got matted rotten wolf pussy on your head, while doing the walk of shame to your uber, after he ravaged your guts and couldn't even give you a soul warming hug and tell you to have a good night. He didn't even feed you the next morning after he fucked you into starvation the night before. He didn't even text you or return your text, for that matter, when you told him you got home safe. He didn't even answer the phone in the days to follow, he didn't even touch the safe on your birthday. Does he even have a safe? Does he even have a place to keep the safe? Is that your King? The man that doesn't care about you; is that your King?

We can't go on like this, ladies. Remy Ma did not do 6 summers up north for us to be out here letting someone's dusty son treat us any kind of way. But you know what I think? I think that the ~~desperate~~ need to be in a relationship these days has some of us women exaggerating the relationships we are in and holding on to men because the pressures of social media have many of you lying to yourself to fit in. With everyone idolizing celebrities and wanting to emulate their lifestyles, having #relationshipgoals without knowing much of anything that goes on behind closed doors, it's no wonder why there are so many fake and failed relationships. Nobody is in it for *real love*, they're in it for *likes* and *looks*. A lot of women are in situationships and relationships, miserable and being fucked over, just to make other women jealous. It's quite absurd if you ask me. There are men that actually shame women for not being in relationships and go out of their way to slander them, in an attempt to make them feel less of a woman because nobody has chosen them. Sadly enough there are women affected by this, so they falsify relationships just to fit in. We have allowed ourselves to be easily triggered and persuaded by what people on social media think about our personal lives. Imagine that, caring about what other people think about your life so much so, you tailor your life to fit other people's expectations, and these are people who haven't even satisfied their own expectations of themselves. Some of us are in relationships with people who have no idea they are in a relationship with us and as a result of that we have created our own hell by exaggerating our place in a man's life. This is exactly how you wind up twerking for the wrong man. Your need to feel or give love has overpowered your common sense. This is why you need real friends that will keep it real with you and keep things in proper perspective for you when you call yourself being in a relationship with someone, when it is really a relationshit. Yes relationshit, that was not a typo. You need friends that will check you on the spot once they see you playing yourself. We hate the blunt friend, but you need that bitch in your life! She is the one that can stop you from twerking for the wrong enword. She is the friend who gives you advice you do not want to hear but need to hear. You will hate her at the moment, but you will love her for it later!

You: I miss him so much.
Her: Girl fuck him.

That's your friend! She will save you from playing yourself because we have all done this time and time again. But then you have some friends that give you the most counterproductive advice. You have to really dig deep into the psyche, hearts and intentions of anyone giving you advice. Some folks will give you advice to push you farther away from achieving your goal and some will give you advice to keep you in a fucked up situation. They take advantage of the fact that you look to them as a sounding board but the sad part is that sometimes people don't have your best interests at heart. They want to keep you at a level that makes them feel better about themselves. Advice disguised as concern and love is the most deceitful shit I've ever experienced in my life. So I don't know about you but when I receive the opinions of others, it doesn't sway me either way. My mind is already made up about how I am going to proceed with the situation. Most times I'm just talking because it's free LOL. I already know what I need to do. But we do have loved ones that want the best for us, but they will get tired of letting you know that you are playing yourself. The shit is exhausting. But we all have gotten so comfortable with a guy and just assumed he would appreciate our "convenience" and not do us dirty or that he was as comfortable with us as we are with him. What a dangerous game we play with our hearts, ladies. But nothing beats that feeling of meeting someone new and the energy being *all that,* and it just flows and you guys getting connected. This is what we all desire, right?

Okay, so we totally skipped steps 1-3. Dine, Date & Decide. But let me get this out of the way, you have the right to take your time and go out with a man several times before you jump in his bed or allow him to jump all in your head. When we need love, we have a tendency to rush things and ignore the red flags. We skip steps 1-3 and go straight to steps 4-6, Dick, Danger, & Delusion. We have to put on our big girl panties and handle all the L's that will come our way when we skip steps in this thang. And baby the L's are coming! Look, the two of you are sexually compatible *and* he got his own place? Oh he ain't fittna go nowhere! We go together whether you know it or not, *sir! This is often how we think after one date at Don Coqui.* We get too comfortable and latch on like those lil koala bears they used to put on our pencils when we were kids. The gag is, he's going to let you get comfortable because convenient pussy is the best pussy. Come on, men live for that! We mistake his availability to sleep with us on the spot for him really liking us and wanting to be with us, don't we? So we start coming over, bringing him food and what not, a bottle of Henny or whatever he likes to drink, always, *"I'm on my way, you need something?"* head ass. You lie up like a couple, binge watching Power and shit, and this goes on for some time; and, despite what we think, we cannot keep up a sexual relationship with anyone without catching feelings, no woman is that cold. I'm sure at this point in my "examples" you know I've experienced making this huge mistake, so here's my truth:

I was once with a guy who was *for everybody,* but I got comfortable with him. He lived close by, I liked him, he was convenient, it was that simple. But here's where I got it fucked up. Over time that convenience lead me to believe that I was special to him. Sometimes even when he wasn't home, I'd get "let in" to his apartment to be able to wait for him until he came home from running the streets. I mean you must be kind of special for a man to let you in his crib while he's not home, right? I'd always spend the night and before leaving the next day we would make plans to "get up" later in the week. My spot was secured, *that's what I felt.* But let me touch on something that comfortability and convenience will blind you from. I was blinded from the fact that this man never *ever* made plans to take me anywhere. Now, in my entire dating career, I had never been in a situationship or relationship with a man that didn't take me out and do things with and for me. Yes, you ruined my life, you rat bastard; but, I had some great memories. It wasn't all bad or I wouldn't have stuck around that long. We went places and created many memories outside of the bedroom. I would never consider dating a man that didn't make plans to do things with me and *for me.* I have no interest in a pillow prince, someone that just wants to lay up with me. So how did I wind up falling for one and becoming a pillow princess? I recognized my feelings for him had grown beyond Netflix and chill. I saw where it was going and I didn't stop it, even when I found myself laying on top of him like he was Melvin and I was Juanita in Baby Boy talking about, *"hold me... tighterrr."* Yawl know the scene when she threw Tyrese out the house and felt bad after? Whatever the case, there was no turning back. Here I was, laid up with a man I knew in my heart would never be able to give me anything I deserved, not even a friendship, yet no matter what the day brought, my night would always end with me knocking on his door. I was the poster child for homie lover friend. But the lie detector test determined even that was a lie as I looked up one day and he was getting married! I wasn't a friend to him. I wasn't shit to him apparently! I had no clue that he was even seriously dating someone else as much time as we spent together. A small community of people, mainly his peers, knew about our "relationship" so when he got married, they reached out to me, asking if I was okay. *I was not*, not for a long time after that. I felt humiliated, stupid, once again. Yaya, how did you slip like this? I believed my own hype that's how. *He ain't going nowhere, all this good-good he getting, all this convenience, where is he going?* I had to hold that Big L like Harlem. But see, when you don't know what you want or if you are unaware of your value, anybody can put a bow on a piece of shit and present it to you like it's a prize. You fall into a cycle of complacency and laziness and that's what I did. He was my Lazy Love. He put in no effort at all. But I knew I wanted to feel some love, some male companionship, and he was there. But I should have known, when he never made plans with me, that I didn't mean anything to him. He never gave a shit about me unless I was in his bed. And then when he began to treat me funny and started getting a little sassy at the mouth with me, low key mean at that, I knew something was going on, but I would have never expected it to be something of this magnitude, *married?* Slap a 27 piece on my head and call me Cora! It hurt like hell because I gave him no reason to ever not keep it real with me or treat me like a nobody. Or maybe I did? But while I was doing all of that *"wondering what are we"* he knew exactly what we were...*nothing*, because he was giving his all to someone else and he got married right on top of my feelings for him, straight fuck your couch, Charlie Murphy! He posted pics all over social media, had children with her and lived his best life all the while not giving a fuck about the love he knew I had for him. He knew how I felt about him because I told him. I'm expressive in that way. But I blame myself because I had no business exaggerating my place in this man's life. I had no business settling for hard dick and bubble gum, because that had *never* been my style. My *fuck you pay me* game was always real. But the moment I went against the grain of how I normally do things I got played. But you live to play yourself another day, right? It took me a long time to heal from that traumatic event not so much because of me being heartbroken but because I was really disappointed in myself. I lowered my standards and got dissed. I had it fucked up. But I had to forgive myself for allowing someone to use me in that way, and it's sometimes harder to forgive yourself than it is to forgive others. But God don't play about me, his marriage failed miserably but that's another story that I don't care enough about to expound on. Time began to heal my wounds and as usual I got back on my feet again, paying more attention this time. I had come so far. I wasn't the woman I was, but I was not perfect, you feel me? So I wasn't exempt from getting played or making mistakes but this time around I wasn't going to sit in it and wallow. I wasn't going to make excuses or throw pity parties. I wasn't going to let it go too far or consume me. That was a mistake I used to make constantly. I would sit in the pain for so damn long, feeling sorry for myself, for what? I wasn't about to do that anymore, so I owned my part in this, learned from it, got stronger because of it, and kept it moving! The climate we are living in is all side bitches, hoes, unfaithful men, outside babies, you name it. I'm a 90s R&B kind of love, living in a City Girl world. It's difficult finding love in this trifling ass climate. Everybody wants you to "come over" and chill. One time was enough for me. I didn't want to be in any man's house unless we were in a relationship. That's the way it had always been until I let ole boy play me. I didn't want to wind up on the Summer Jam screen again. I didn't want to wind up standing on the sidelines while yet another man chose someone over me. But I also had another aha! moment as I began to reflect on things. I realized that it wasn't because I was *unworthy*, as the reason why these men were moving like this, it was two things. For one, the men I had come across were broken as well and I wasn't whole yet. I attracted men that only had the bandwidth to cater to that one part of me that was unfulfilled at the time. I only had a fraction to offer and got a fraction in return. Though I wanted the whole package, realistically I could only operate from that one part of me that wasn't healed. And two, I was too good at being the cool girl. The down for whatever girl. The no drama girl. I'd flip over a table if someone messed with me, but as long as I was getting what I wanted, I was pretty lowkey. This is very important if you are that girl. I want you to stop being that girl right now! I was "the cool girl." I didn't make a fuss about much, I didn't sweat shit, I didn't ask for what I wanted or deserved, I didn't argue or fight, I didn't ask questions. I just went with the flow and expected them to appreciate that part of me and reward me for it. In turn, they all assumed that they could absorb all my air and not have to give me anything because I didn't ask and probably wouldn't trip off shit. I was the homie lover friend. *"Nah Ayana cool, she's not gonna mind."* I allowed this, so I'm going to hold those L's once again. Just call me LL Cool A. I was out here living wrong! Being the cool chick is not what's up. Why nobody ain't tell me? Well I'm here to tell *you*, you better open your mouth and say what you feel, woman. Ask for what you deserve and most importantly show people how to treat you by what you are willing to accept. I was willing to accept nothing and anything at the same time. A cool fool. Fuck being the cool girl, say what you want and carry yourself in that manner. But here I was again, another lesson learned.

And listen, I understand that it's not all about being in a serious relationship all the time, but you have to know who to play these games of convenience with, ladies. I'm not suggesting that you can't have a healthy *situationship*. Sometimes we don't want any strings attached, we just want to do our thing, and I am here for it... IF you can handle it. I'm merely warning you against the dangers of wanting more but settling for less and acting like everything's cool as to not push a man away. Also, just because you are not in a committed relationship with someone does not mean that he doesn't have to treat you with respect. So what you are in a "situationship" or casually dating him. The energy and time that you are putting into this person is worthy of respect, regardless. You are still a person, a human, a woman and you don't have to be some man's wife, lady, girlfriend or any other title in order to receive respect from him. Missy Misdemeanor Elliot did not hee-hee hee-hee how, for us to be getting played like we ain't worth shit. It was way past time to act accordingly. I could no longer go from being a woman of substance to being dismissed, like an object or something to play with. I recognized myself as a loving woman early on, but now I had to tap into my discernment. I wasn't about to change who I was. I just needed to change who I gave my love to. We know in our heart of hearts that this is not the way to go. You can't fuck a man into a relationship, and you can't suck him into loving you. This is not going to end well. You know you have to do something about this. That is when you get that nagging feeling in your gut to ask him that dreadful question. You know the question, the one that puts an end to most, if not all, relationships of convenience, aka situationships. The dreadful question of:

"So, what are we?"

Doh! My heart just sank for you! Jesus Christopher Wallace.

Hint: If you have to ask then you already know the answer. You know it's a wrap the moment you let those words leave your mouth, so you don't ask because you don't want to lose him, and now you're stuck having to settle. Now you're stuck after you gave this man all of you in exchange for only a *few inches* of himself in return. Literally—a few inches. The moment you try to inconvenience things with your emotions, it's over. We must be real with ourselves that if not for convenience, we would not get so much of this man's time. Keep in mind, he is not making time for you, don't get it twisted. *You are convenient.* He's not going out of his way, nor do you make him go out of his way to see you. And when he's simply had enough or comes across another woman, he wants to spend time with, a woman that *makes him chase her a little* bit perhaps, he's going to take off running in the other direction, after her. All the curve balls will start coming at you, and you will be in denial at first, so you will chase him some more, try to fit into his schedule, try to keep things going. You will not want to accept that your twerking days are numbered. You will question why he's being so distant, after all you were convenient, you didn't give no headaches or demands, you didn't ask anything of him, and why would he want to throw all that away? What happened? *Nothing happened,* beloved, you were just out here twerking for the wrong enword. The right one wouldn't dispose of you or ghost you or cowardly take advantage of your love knowing he was going to waste your time until his wedding day. You gave it all to someone that didn't want nor deserve you. But looka here, men are only savages when they aren't ready to settle down or when you are clearly not the one. You cannot force them nor should you waste your time trying to be "the one" for him. The right one will make plans outside of the bedroom. He will jam up your weekend before your girls do. He will occupy your Saturday evenings well into your Sunday mornings. He will meet with you after work, he will invite you to run errands with him, he will take you to the cookouts and gatherings. He will spend time with you at your place in your surroundings. Every time he sees you it doesn't have to end with you having to give him sex. He is not pressed, he got you, he wants you and he will have you when he wants to because he earned it you understand how that works? You won't have to force it or wonder. You won't feel inadequate or ashamed. He will earn you and you will feel the difference between him and when a man treats you like a convenience. He will make plans all the time to keep you interested and satisfied. He is also a grown man who values his own time so he's not going to play games with you just for fuck boys sake. He will value you and you will know it, energy does not lie. But we keep giving ourselves away to men who don't value us. We hold on to the hope that one day he will change, value us, see something in us to make them act right. But baby, hope is just a rope that we all hang ourselves from time and time again. You must take responsibility for your actions. Cut the rope, cut your losses, and move on even with the tears falling down your face, even while it hurts like hell, even as you watch the man you love exchange vows for everyone to see, you gotta get ahead of that hurt and move on. You gotta transfer that energy off of you and return it to the sender. Don't carry that shit with you. But if all you want is a cut buddy or something temporary then your actions must reflect such. You can't fully invest in or cater to a man that you don't see a future with or one that you're not sure wants a future with you. You will end up with your heart broken time and time again and baby girl you are too precious to be hurting all the time. Mascara is too damn expensive to be ruining it over somebody's dusty son. Don't beat yourself up about it either. In my case, I realized after the fact that he was nothing to be upset about not being chosen by. I looked back and realized that I was dating a broken man who didn't really love himself. He's still a womanizer til this day, jumping in one relationship after another, never giving himself an opportunity to be alone because he doesn't like himself, I concluded. In fact, years later he apologized to me for how he treated me and admitted to me that he could never be in anything serious with me because I am not a woman that he can control and that he chooses to be with women whose minds he can manipulate. He of course is now separated from his wife and has another poor unsuspecting girlfriend while going through a divorce, while he raises two small children under 5 years old, with his wife. Phew chile the ghetto! So ladies the lesson in that is, never force yourself on any man or try to make something work that clearly isn't meant for you. God knows what he's doing when he's blocking you and *your him* from connecting on a higher level. Most of the time when a man mistreats you, it's not because of you, but because of the insecurities and discrepancies they are dealing with inside. Motherfuckas be flawed as hell out here sis but will try to make it seem as if you are the problem and as a result, that is why he mistreats you, don't sleep. But lesson learned right? Forgive yourself, but don't do that shit again. The results will be the same, time and time again! You are worth way more than hard dick and bubble gum, I don't care what anybody says or tries to make you believe. Look sis, I don't know what else to tell you, but I don't think a man really cares about you if he isn't taking care of you. Men take care of what they love. They are kind to who they care about, they want to flaunt the woman that they are claiming. He's not going to keep you inside. So if he's not taking you out, he's not spending quality time with you, he's not doing anything with you but fucking you? Eh, I'd bet my life on it that you don't mean as much to him as you think you do. Close your legs and go home. You deserve so much better than this.

The moral of the story is this:
Never treat a <u>thing</u> like a King.

4 WHEN A RICH NI**A WANTS YOU....

I've dated all kinds of men. I've dated 9 to 5 guys, I've dated dope boys. I've dated so called, "Good Guys" and a plethora of "Bad Boys." The only difference between all these men was their criminal record or lack thereof, so when others try to convince me that one enword is better than another, I just say: girl bye. Don't get caught up in that good guy, bad boy rhetoric. It's not real. It's all perception. Truth be told, most of the so-called good guys I've dated had worse behavior and personalities than the bad boys. The ones I've dated all had a chip on their shoulder, they felt as if I should worship them because they have never been to jail, or because they had a *"good job."* They had this air about them that said, I am better than. It's sort of like how the Pick Me women turn their noses up at "Bad Bitches", you know? So I say just go for the man that respects himself, is a hustler, and knows how to feed himself and his family. Good Guy image is only limited to men that have never been in the streets. That doesn't mean he is in fact a good guy and isn't capable of being an abusive, bitch ass, unsupportive dick head. Nor does it mean a bad boy is a bad person and that he will beat you and go in and out of jail. It's all stereotypical. But now as an adult, coming into myself and realizing I was ready to try this settling down thing the so called "right way" I knew I wanted neither of those. I could care less if you had a felony or a PhD. I just needed a good solid man on my arm. I thought the answer to all my dreams would be to snag a rich man, not by hook or crook but by divine intervention. And when I say rich, I'm not talking hood rich, been there done that. I'm talking about a made man, connected! I thought having a rich man would be the answer to all my problems. I wanted some handsome, rich enword to sweep me off my feet and whisk me away into happily ever after. I made the executive decision that from then on, I was going to cry in a penthouse instead of the projects. I figured if I'm going to twerk for an enword, why not let it be a rich one? At least he could afford to tip me my worth. So as luck would have it, and me knowing how the universe works, I willed such an experience into my world.

Allow me to tell you a short story:

Picture it, Manhattan 2017. I went to an intimate industry event with a friend who is in "the industry" and the next morning I get a call that the record label owner wants to know who I am. At this point I have been single and totally celibate for a year. I feel great, free, and fine about myself. Life is good. I'm working on some new projects, moving with a lighter load—the Queen is straight! I'm ready to go mingle, get some phone numbers, date, text, waste a few dudes times, whatever it is you're supposed to do when you meet people. I had an entirely new outlook this time. I was honest enough with myself to admit that I wanted more, I wanted something real. I was dating with a purpose. No more frontin' like I didn't want to be in a relationship. No more wasting time in these situations, holleration, hateration in the dancer-ree. I planned on being up front about my expectations with any man I met, and that was that. I was feeling confident about myself and my life and had every intention of spreading that energy all up and through these New York streets. I earned the right to a good man, I deserved it, I prayed on it, I set my life up to attract the good in all people not just men. I did the work, I took care of myself and rid myself of all baggage. *Well most.* I healed the broken parts of my life that attracted these narcissistic fuck boys and became a serial optimist. My self-esteem was high and the void I had in my life that allowed men to only love me a little bit was filled. Now you had to love me whole because I was whole. I was no longer a fragment, a fraction, a piece, broken. Being celibate was a great thing. It calmed my flesh down, I focused on Ayana, and I learned to live without male contact. I got to know myself more and more after the demise of each relationship.

The ending of each relationship revealed a deeper need and a different me. My discipline was crazy now! My discernment even more fire. My solitude was so sweet! I became unapologetic about my wants and needs and had no problem walking away from anyone that wasn't with the program. I had a list of non-negotiables, as every woman should have. You know, a handful of things that a man must have, or all bets are off. I was equipped with confidence, self-love, and wisdom. I was ready. My mind was just different, everything was just different. I was no longer a little girl in need, I was a grown ass woman. I was tired of the lonely nights and tired of convincing myself that I was happily single. I was ready to build with and enter a *consensual*, committed relationship with someone worthy of my wisdom and womanisms. I make it a point to say *consensual* because some of us be in whole relationships unbeknownst to our partners. *Just saying.* You gotta let folks know when they are in a relationship with you sometimes. I let go of the notion that all men cheated and had a secret family stashed somewhere. I stopped fearing love. I was ready to take a chance like a big girl! I grew up and found the courage to trust love one more time! I realized that the decisions these men made to not honor me as a woman was not a reflection of the Queen Yaya, but of the peasant mind state they lived in. It was *they* who were intimidated by my potential to take them to higher heights with my love, my being, (that they clearly were not ready for... *at least not with me*) so in turn they tried to cut me off at the knees and knock me down because I was too tall for them. This is not me gloating—this is a fact. So please do yourself a favor, before you beat yourself up wondering what you did wrong and why he treated you that way, understand that his behavior is not a reflection of how he sees you but how he views himself. Hurt people, hurt people! So this time around, I really took my time and opened myself up to receiving love. And to my surprise without even looking or trying too hard, the universe sent me exactly what I was looking for, filthy rich, 6ft ...ok *he was like 5ft 10, closer to 5ft 11*...and handsome. We will refer to him as

"Jay." Jay appeared to be even keeled, something I surely wasn't used to in most of the men I previously dated. You know with my track record I decided to be cautious, sit back, and let him show me what he needed to show me before I got too comfortable. I dined, dated, and decided. I did the steps, yawl. I was secure in myself, so I felt no need to rush. I wanted to make sure his soul was right, and his spirit was intact, ya feel me? I had experienced too much to allow anyone to come into my life and shake my core. At this point in my life, I found peace, and I was solid. I was the shit! And I began attracting a different caliber of men. But still, I had to double check his story, make sure there weren't any wife and kids somewhere because he could easily afford to have 3 or 4 families stashed away in different parts of the world. I had to make sure there weren't any silly baby mamas or any females in his life that felt as if they would and could pull rank over me. I was done playing nice and dealing with "enwords" and their illegitimate relationships. I was done being "understanding" of these enwords and their "baggage." I was no longer the cool girl. I don't care what I accepted in the past. I wasn't accepting none of that shit now! I wasn't dealing with disrespectful baby mother's that suffered from delusions of Grandeur or the fuck boys who entertained them and allowed them to act up to feed their bum ass egos. I had to make sure he wasn't tainted from his childhood and trying to dump his trauma on me. I had to make sure he was healed. I asked the questions, I did the work. There was so much I had learned and had to unravel before even thinking about giving my heart or body to anybody. I had arrived and was no longer settling for anything less than what I could reciprocate. I had a lot to offer, and I wanted the same in return, with interest!

This man appeared to be the real deal, unattached, thank God, smart, classy, and well-traveled. He had great taste in damn near everything, clothes, food, books, you name it. He was a dream come true. But finding what I thought was the man of my dreams wasn't a cause for celebration. You would think that after all I'd been through,

I would be happy. No, I was scared fucking shitless. I was not in the mood for industry shenanigans, so because of his status, I was extra cautious, but he seemed to be smitten by me, and it took him no time to try to lock me into a relationship which I found a bit nerve wracking. I chalked it up to when a man knows what he wants, he doesn't hesitate to go get it. Sounds about right, right? But I didn't want to be another bitch on his hit list. I didn't want to be treated like a groupie or anything like that. I didn't want to have to come out of retirement and slice and dice his apple head for trying to treat me any old kind of way, so I did all I could to make sure this wouldn't be the case by taking my time. I didn't let him buy me or force me into a relationship. But the more time he put into me and the extremes he went to show me that he was serious, the more my pessimism began to fade away. I made it clear that I was dating with a purpose, he agreed that he too was looking for *the one.* After a while, I started to take him seriously based on his consistency, but I still wasn't sold because a man can be consistent and do so many things for you and *with you* and still not want a commitment. They can treat you like you're their girl but the moment you catch feelings or have an opinion on something they do, they will remind you quickly, *"we are not in a relationship, you are not my girl."* You can spend nights, spend time, meet his mother, his homies, his uncle, his kids, have raw sex every night, cuddle and cook for him, be there for him, hold his hand at his Nana's funeral and ride in the family car, but until the man has that conversation with you and asks you to be his woman? Don't you get suspicious. Do not assume. Do not for one second think that you are his girl. So I still waited for a conversation and some understanding initiated by him before I was able to breathe a little. And honestly, I wasn't even pressed for it. I was really learning to go with the flow and not have any expectations, and it felt so good, so adult like. I was like *yaaaaz this is how you're supposed to finesse this relationship shit!* Make them wait, make them earn it, let them prove it to you and carry on with your life unbothered. And so one day, he whisked me off to his condo in Miami for a few days, and we had a ball. One thing is for sure, you can see how compatible you are with someone while on vacation. We had a really nice time and then one night he hit me with _thee_ conversation. "*I want us to be exclusive; just me and you; see where this goes. I want you to be my Queen.*" he said to me one night in the VIP section of club Liv. I still didn't trust it. We were on a champagne campaign all night, and he was drunk, we both were. We were living La vida Loca that entire weekend, so I shrugged him off, told him to knock it off and continued enjoying my flashy ass night surrounded by his celebrity friends. But he woke up the next morning and in all sobriety, looked me dead in my eyes and said *I remember what I said last night, be my Queen; me and you; let's do this.* This was all I needed to hear to let my guard down. Finally, I got a grown ass man that said what he wanted and proved it with his actions. As the months went by, I of course began to spend lots of time at his home. He would cook for me, we would laugh and talk a lot, it was nice. We spent so much time together, he suggested we meet one another's children, so we planned a playdate, took them ice skating, and started to do grown people things. This was new to me, and I began to open up in ways I hadn't before. New levels, new devils though. We started making plans to do things months in advance, which made me feel secure. Even though he started traveling a lot, it was cool because I was traveling for business as well. It was sexy, both of us flying back into NY, me showing up with my luggage to my man in the kitchen cheffing up some healthy meals, while I shake up our drinks and put the music on, and both of us talking about our trips. It was the life I had imagined for myself. Finally it was here.

But then a shift happened, you know when the vibe just kind of switches up on you a little bit? It was "something," but not enough to ask him any questions but enough to awaken my paranoia. I continued to twerk for him because *he said* this is what *he* wanted; *he* asked me to be his woman and *he* showed how serious he was by the time and effort *he* put into the relationship. I continued to let him show me how much he wanted to be with me. I didn't do the most, I just enjoyed a man for once and let him lead, let him drive, you know? He made time for me, he wined and dined me in a way that only a rich man could, and when we made love, I felt connected. But something different was floating around our love. Something wasn't quite right. Something was missing. My spidey senses started tingling and from prior experience, I began to pay even more attention to him. I documented patterns and moves. There were times when he would get really down and depressed. I knew that he had lost his mother really young, and I knew that before me he had ended a long-term relationship. He would zone out a lot. I was learning him and what I gathered was that all of the things he did with me were a distraction from the pain he was trying to hide. In hindsight, I came to the realization that a "man like him" just needed a woman in his life for comfort and nothing else. Any woman would do. I just so happen to be the woman for now. I felt that way once the honeymoon phase was over. He did what he had to do to get me, and then he stopped doing even the small things once I was locked in and showing emotion. He stopped making me feel as if I was a priority. I found myself doing most of the calling and planning of dates when it used to be him. No matter where he was in the world, he would call, email if he had to, just to make sure we had reservations somewhere when he got home and included our kids. And when I would go to his home, he was always on "business calls" or he was tired. Most nights were quiet, no longer filled with music playing, playlists battles, love making, sweet kisses, and talks on his penthouse balcony. He began to make me feel as if I was being bothersome when I tried to show him affection. Perhaps he's stressed, I mean after all, his life is filled with making deals all day. Though in my heart, he was showing me the clear signs of not wanting to be with me, I didn't understand why he wouldn't want to be with me anymore. I didn't change, in fact I improved, opened up more and became more loving once he convinced me he was staying around. After all, he is the one that chased and pursued me and was relentless at making me his woman, and I was good to him, as good as he was to me. Now that I was open, he was falling back. It didn't make sense. What man would lie about wanting to be in a relationship with a woman when he had nothing to gain from lying to her? I gave him a pass even as I began to fade into his background. Yes, I *continued* to twerk for him when I knew in my heart I needed to reevaluate this relationship. I felt him slipping away, and it did not feel good at all. I don't think I've ever experienced the slippation of a ni**a out of my life in my entire history of niggadom. Then I convinced myself it was me and some old insecurities crept back in, so I pepped talked myself: "*Relax Ayana you are just paranoid.*" He even said the "L" word to me several times at this point. But by then, his emotions were all over the place, one day he was loving, the next totally distant, cold even. I began to suspect that he was running from something or possibly seeing someone else. Was it because of me? Was I not what and who he thought I would be? Was there something in his past haunting him? I asked him if I made him unhappy and he said no, sealed it with a kiss, and told me to relax, *"we good babe."* But I wasn't convinced. Time went on, and he began showing signs of us being anything but good. He would go on tour and not call for a whole week, something he would never do. I was used to him calling me from any part of the world he was in, sending me pictures, and telling me he wished I was with him. He became emotionally and mentally unavailable more and more, each time he went away and came back, which was something I could not and <u>would not accept</u> in a relationship. You see I'm the kind of woman that needs love and affection from my man. I need you on me, I need to know and feel your love always. I never want to have to question how you feel about me. I began to feel really fucking uneasy guys. Yet I stayed because *he* wanted this relationship, *he* had asked on many occasions for me to take him seriously and *finally* I did. Why would he have cold feet now when it was his idea?

I was torn between holding on to my dream guy or holding on to my integrity. He was no longer the same person, it was as if the mask he wore to get me was beginning to fall off. He began making me feel as if I was just a *"catch and kill"* that he could just invite over for a good time. I indeed became the very thing I tried to avoid, *another bitch on his hit list.* He became *way too busy* and unable to see me. And you know that nobody is busier than a motherfucka that's not into you. One thing became very clear, he was not into me anymore. Things changed significantly without warning. I learned a hard lesson dealing with this man. People can choose to no longer deal with you, and they do not owe you an explanation at all. It's fucked up and tacky as hell, but it's a harsh truth. Love is a gamble. You can do all the research and be as cautious as you want but you never know who you're going to wind up with. It's up to you to believe what's in front of you or make excuses. Time reveals all things, and it's on you to waste your time or move forward. Guess what I did? I continued wasting time. Never, ever do that! Your gut doesn't lie! I could wreck my brain trying to figure out what happened between us, but since he wasn't man enough to communicate with me, I said fuck 'em because what that said to me was that he was not genuine, and I was not going to try and convince myself otherwise. If nothing else, I learned to believe a person when they show me who they are. I no longer made excuses. What it all boiled down to is this right here: I stayed around longer than I should have because he chose me, and no one has ever quite chosen or chased me before. **Let that sink in.**

Do you *choose yourself* at this point? Do you hold on? Misery soon consumed me because I was playing myself trying to force this thing. I didn't chase him but I damn sure did a light jog. I didn't like how that felt. It wasn't my style. I learned a long time ago to never pretend like you don't know how a man feels about you. Be honest with yourself.

He was showing me how he felt about me. He didn't care about me, *"I love you"* was a lie, it was all a lie. I was not going to allow this man that pursued me so heavily to treat me like I wasn't shit suddenly. I needed and deserved better. He wasn't the one, it was time to admit it. He wasn't deep enough, he wasn't passionate enough, he didn't love me enough, he didn't turn me on enough, he didn't impress me or make me want to follow his lead. I didn't feel safe or protected by him. I didn't feel needed or adored by him. It was all so shallow. He didn't open up to me the way I needed and in turn he didn't allow me to want to open up to him the way I would have liked to have with the man I am supposed to be building with. That was the feeling I couldn't quite put my finger on early on. But I swung on the hope rope, hoping not to get choked. My only mistake was staying longer than I should have and not going with my gut. There was a reason why I was so cautious and didn't jump out the window with him in the beginning. I looked around his big, beautiful penthouse and realized how empty it was, just like his soul. *The man who seemingly had everything really had nothing to offer me.* I could clearly date someone nowhere near as rich as him and receive so much more. Ciara did not 1,2 step her way into Russell Wilson's life for me to be over here tossing and turning over some man that clearly no longer held an interest in me. I had to get over myself and him.

So our last time out together was because of him *possibly* feeling guilty of treating me so disposable. He flew into town just in time for the 4th of July, and like the old days, gave me his card, told me to get tickets for us to watch the fireworks on top of the Empire State Building, and to make lunch reservations at Tavern on the Green. Reluctantly I went, as my daughter was out of town with her father, and I didn't want to be home alone. Lunch was awkward as he spent most of his time on business calls while I kept his 6-year-old son company. After the fireworks, we headed out of the Empire State Building where I attempted to catch a cab to go home, but his son pleaded for me to come home with them. I went along for closure purposes. I had to feel the ending, so I could move on, and I knew I'd feel it once I entered his home. The ride home was silent. I knew I was done when we put his son to bed and he summoned me to the bedroom. I prayed he didn't touch me, I turned my back to him, and tucked my hands between my legs like I was cold. He didn't even try. The next morning I tiptoed across his marble floors and took my ass home for good. I was heartbroken to say the least. I didn't appreciate being handled that way, not when I was minding my damn business, celibate, and sucker free just to get bamboozled into a relationship by a narcissist. Of course he tried to reel me back in, perhaps only because I chose to walk away. With the utmost *disrespect,* I declined. Because you know how these enwords are, they only want you when you're not there, but my happiness did not have a price on it. No amount of lavish living could replace the sunshine that my spirit held. And to keep it all the way real, he didn't even lavish me that much. I had received much more from men with much less, so that was whatever. **I chose myself** and never felt freer. Once a woman chooses herself over a man, she is never coming back and besides, there's a statute of limitations in getting over someone. I wasn't about to sit in a dark corner over some man who couldn't recognize he had the whole world in his possession, and he lost it. I wasn't about to question was I good enough and bust my brain trying to figure out why he didn't want to be with me anymore. I was not about to try to convince some man to treat me better and to love me right. Fuck him, he didn't deserve my pain or tears. His *rejection* of me was God's protection. Or maybe he simply decided I was not the one, and he was too much of a coward to say so. No matter how dope you are, people do have a right to <u>not</u> choose you. I realized I didn't need a man to choose me, as long as I *always* chose myself. I enjoyed the short but sweet experience of living the lifestyles of the rich and famous but decided I would rather live the lifestyle of inner peace and genuine love... *of course with some change to spare* because let's not get crazy here. Now, when I'm looking at men and their shit-meter, I am more so impressed by humility, integrity, kindness, compassion and genuity as opposed to money, degrees, and status. I can't tell you how many times I sat across from him at a fancy restaurant, drinking some exotic wine or champagne, and eating some she-she-foo-foo shit, feeling morally poor as he talked about himself and humble-bragged about everything he did or owned. I don't know how many times I laid on his expensive ass mattress, wanting to just sink into the foam and disappear. And, though I stand firm in my wants and desires of a financially stable gentleman, I know there must be more attached to the man than money and status. I'm too deep and passionate to ever be in a relationship built off material things alone. But I had to experience him to know what it was I really needed in a man going forward. Having a man with a few dollars is cool. But there has to be some sort of balance. I don't know if someone reading this is in a relationship of sorts with a man that has money; yet they feel unfulfilled, choosing to stay for the "pretty picture," knowing they want more out of the relationship but would rather stay to see what they can get. Just trust and believe that just like you attracted him, you can attract a better version of him. Money doesn't mean shit if you're piss poor morally. Don't be afraid to give up the good in exchange for the great! Because sometimes what we think we want is no good for us at all. It's worth experiencing just so you know what you *don't want* and need, but don't stay in your mistake because you are too afraid to admit to yourself that you made the wrong decision, or because it looks good It's okay to admit things to yourself and move on. Yes, you were burned; just call it a lesson learned!

The moral of the story is this:
Your soul should <u>never</u> be for sale. **Never.**

Message!

So many of us women have high expectations, and we get severely disappointed when "He" doesn't live up to the hype. But the issue is not him, but the expectations YOU put on your him. Nine times out of ten, *he* came with all he had to offer. Yet, we always want to look past what he shows us. We make up scenarios and situations in our heads, and we make excuses for him. Then we put all of this effort and energy into maintaining the lie we told ourselves and get mad at him for not living up to our delusion. We have to stop doing this to ourselves, ladies. We gotta call a thing a thing as Auntie Iyanla says. You gotta understand that this man that you so desperately want to be your King will never present himself as such. He is all he will ever be... I'ma say that again. **He is all he will ever be.** And we have to love ourselves enough to move on from any situation that doesn't represent how we feel about ourselves inside—period. So many times we compromise ourselves and the life we really want for a temporary fix. We get into situations that we know has no happy ending; situations that we know will lead us down a dark path; we stay in situations because we rather put on a front for people who don't care and try to make them happy rather than make ourselves happy. We care too much about what people think, we give a fuck when its not even our turn. A lot of you are in situations that you don't want to be in but the pressure to perform is too great, your captive audience is hanging on to your every move.

Not to mention that nagging wanting and yearning inside of us that catapults us into a level of stupidity and blindness that we gotta literally fight our way out of. It can take months, sometimes years to recover from one mistake, one that we didn't have to make. We go against the grain, we go against what we know is right, we go against what we know we shouldn't be doing for that temporary fix and the pusher man is right there luring you in telling you it's going to be okay. He doesn't care about how you will be affected, all he cares about is getting you high and watching you crawl to him when you're feeling low. It doesn't have to be this way ladies. You don't have to go through shit to learn a lesson all the time. Simply use your head and not your heart. With age comes wisdom and I can't say women over 30 or over 40 or whatever need to know better. But we have to learn from our mistakes, or we are doomed to repeat them. You know how something is going to end before it starts. Stop playing yourself ladies. Guard Your

Spirit
BE GREAT!!!!!!!!!!!!!!!!

5 R.A.N

(Real Ass Nia)**

I wish I knew then what I know now, don't you? But do yourself a favor. Don't call yourself young and dumb. Don't beat yourself up. You were simply *uninformed,* and you did what you thought was the right thing to do. Had you been schooled on the importance of learning more about a man's family history and pathology before considering being in a relationship you wouldn't have gone through half the things you had to experience. You didn't know about red flags and non-negotiables. You had to learn the hard way through trial and error. You took a lot of L's and kissed a lot of frogs because you weren't taught. Your father was not there, or maybe he was but did not serve as the greatest example of what to expect from a man. For me, I used to look at everyone as temporary, thinking that at some point they leave. *They always leave.* Sometimes, I behaved in a manner to make them leave, so I wouldn't be disappointed and hurt by inevitable abandonment. Sometimes, I held on too tight forcing them to run away from me because I was suffocating them. Sometimes, I simply exaggerated my place in their life because the only thing I had the energy for was dreaming. And sometimes, I just simply pushed them away. I didn't believe any relationship was real. I looked at the people around me, the men who cheated or had an overall low performance, and figured someone was settling. I figured I was going to find out about some woman. I was going to find out he really didn't love me. I was going to find out he lied. I was going to find out something that was going to break my heart. It just seemed so hard and not worth it, I often would rather be single than to endure such pain. I cried a whole lot of years and suffered quietly. I fought for love from men instead of fighting to love myself.

But then one day my soul just opened up. Something came over me and I said, "*Ayana, baby girl, what is you doing? Ain't no way you can truly believe that you are unworthy of respect and everlasting love. Who taught you that? Why do you believe that?*" I had no answer. Have you ever had that happen to you? One day you just wake up different. So, I flipped that energy around and returned to sender. I started loving on myself, and it made folks uncomfortable. The ones that benefited from my lack of self-love were the ones that began to fall out of my circle once I no longer tolerated their bullshit. It took years to love myself the right way. It took time to become unapologetic in my attitude and moves. It took time to undo all the damage I caused and allowed. I no longer cared who my self-love blinded or offended. This was how it was going down from here on out. I knew better, and I began to do better; so, when you learn you teach. I can pass this wisdom down to my daughter so that she, God willing, won't make the mistakes I did. So, you see, my pain wasn't in vain at all. A lot of shit broke my heart, but it fixed my vision; so, I ain't too mad, you feel me?

The fight is hard and there isn't much you can do when you are up against a generation of men whose mother's dragged them up instead of raising them up, coddled them and turned the other cheek, then sent them out into the world to be someone's boyfriend, father, or husband. There isn't much that we can do when these father's constantly abandon these young men, leaving them bitter and uninformed on how to treat a woman and how to be a man. They too have to learn on their own; and unfortunately, women become their crash test dummies until they get it right. Then the world is left with a whole heap of heartbroken and angry women; because men are running through here like the Tazmanian devil tearing up shit in search of love and the home their parents did not provide. This is why it's so important to take self-inventory and really heal yourself before stepping out into the world calling yourself dating someone or getting into a relationship. You don't know who is using you or who truly wants to be with you.

A lot of men are out here heartbroken behind the fact that they didn't have a father, or their mother didn't set a good example, and they take it out on women. But you also have men that go in the opposite direction, and they strive to be better men than their fathers were, and they adore women because of what they saw their mothers go through. Those are my heroes, and I applaud their strength and courage in acknowledging their pain, fixing it, and paying it forward by becoming great fathers and great husbands and/or mates. But so many men are left to fend for themselves. So many of us are so broken and uninformed, hence, all the toxic relationships we all have experienced or witnessed our loved one's experience.

Unfortunately, when I was younger, I had to experience domestic violence, and nobody told me this young man had mental issues, *forreal forreal.* I later found out he did a stint in the G building in Brooklyn. It made sense how he could one day be so sweet and the next, he was trying to throw me down a flight of stairs or out of a moving car on the Jackie Robinson. All in all, I never gave "mental health" a second thought after him. I was too busy trying to survive. I started to look more into the mental health of the men I talked to as I got older, and after seeing so many women die at the hands of a mentally challenged man. My own mental health wasn't up to par, so I began paying attention to everything around me. After surviving my own mental gymnastics, I wanted to steer clear of any man that would trigger that beast in me. I started to pay attention to patterns and asked the men I started dating about their families and children. I was interested in a man's pathology, family, and thoughts. I began to listen more and ride the vibrations of men. It saved me from quite a few nut cases to be honest, like this one guy who I shall affectionately call *"basement boy"* because yes, he lived in a basement, and he was always trying to invite me over for "a date." Basement boy always wanted to argue which alarmed me. Out the gate he found something to argue or fuss about— like dude I'm not about to have relationship problems with someone I'm not in a relationship with. Where are you getting this idea that it's okay to argue all the time? Oh, how did I wind up dating someone that lived in a basement after all I've been through? Well duh, I didn't know he lived in a basement until I got to his house, and he lead me to the side door, and I'm like *"oh my God, Ya you hit a real low point, you dating enwords that live under the stairs now?"* He claimed he owned the house and lived in the basement to save money, but whatever. I don't care what you own I care about this fire hazard we are in right now!

And for the record, I can't call it dating, we only saw each other this one time. Prior to that, we spent lots of time on the phone and facetime, and I gathered from the phone conversations that he was a bit aggressive and confrontational. But it wasn't enough to turn me off at the time. I convinced myself to be cool in this basement and to just see how shit went. Ladies, a word to the wise, fuck seeing how shit goes! If you don't like something, don't do it! But see, my problem was for a *split second* in my dating career, I tried not to come off as being too high maintenance. You know as women, we go through a short phase where we start checking ourselves as the reason why we are single. I let a few people tell me that my standards were too high, and I should be looking for *this* instead of *that,* so I agreed that our first date didn't necessarily need to be at Brooklyn Chop House or Ruth Chris, and we could just talk and chill. That was music to his basic ass ears unbeknownst to me. So when I got there, to my dismay, this man lived in a basement, sneakers everywhere, and of course a big ass flat screen TV if nothing else. This was so not my cup of tea, but I was already there and decided to make the best of the evening. However, it was at that moment I owned my truth. I said you know what Yaya, so what you have standards, so what you are a bit high maintenance, what the hell are you settling for, to make somebody's dusty ass son you barely know feel comfortable in his mediocrity? Nah. Cardi B did not blow a bag on some teeth for us to be out here laid up in somebody's asbestos filled basement for the sake of not coming off as high maintenance.

But here's what happened afterwards. All because I dumbed myself down and dated him in his house on the first date, every time we tried to make plans to go out he would suggest me coming over *again* and then he would get mad when I said no, let's go out. It was such a turn off. I got rid of his ass after a few phone calls once I realized he wasn't trying to spend money on a date. He didn't even know where to take me or how to date me. He began texting me and calling *me* crazy. He was really trying to convince me that I was doing too much by wanting to go out and why couldn't I just come over and chill. This ni**a was really trying to date me in the house. This is why you can't be humble and nice to enwords, for what? I eventually had to block him. He was just angry, basic and cheap for no damn reason. But you see, had I allowed it, we'd be a superhero team! Basement Boy and Basic Bitch, taking over the world and being hashtag relationship goals for all the couples in the world that don't want shit out of life. He would have never considered giving me more because I didn't command it. Nor did he have any more to offer me other than trips under the stairs. And even if he had more to offer and didn't think I was good enough for him to present it to, fuck him either way. No thanks. See, he's definitely the kind of guy that would text me, "I want to see you." To which I would reply, "Okay, make some plans." Then the phone would go silent. Oh! But he will text you again, a week or so later, maybe even longer, talking about "Hey, what's up when I'ma see you." *Boy fuck you.*

Ladies, we have to be very very careful. Some men really have it out for us. They want nothing more than to tear us down from head to toe. When a man doesn't love himself, the damage that he can do to a woman can be deadly, irreversible, unfixable. Once you feel a man playing with your head and your time? You better get the hell out of there fast! Then you have some men that have no shame dating a woman because he's trying to get out his mother's house. There are men that will get a woman pregnant because she has a good job and all he has is good dick to offer. Some of these men are out here looking for 3 hots and a cot. Some men are simply looking for a beautiful thing to conquer and destroy. Know your audience.

Men have a lot of pressure on them now to be rich or to be a baller such as women have pressure on them as well to have a flat tummy, slim waist, and to be a boss bitch with 67 inches of ass. Things have gotten way out of control. It's no longer good enough for a man to work in the post office. Women want you to own the damn post office and men know it. The main reason men go so hard to get money is because it gives them access to any woman they want, correct? I think the pressure applied on today's man to be successful has a lot of men stressed out, bitter, and miserable. And (some) men simply do not have what it takes to keep up or be a part of the game, so they become emotionally detached and miserable, and they take it out on women. They call us hoes and gold diggers for wanting to date men doing better than them. It's a rough game out here, man. I pity the men *and* women trying to keep up with the joneses. That's gotta be a stressful life to live, trying to be something you're not, to become something in order to gain acceptance from folks that don't even care. If a person cannot accept you for you or love you for you, why bother entertaining them? Some men seek out women who they feel will stay and try to fix them, accept them, and/or build them up. These women turn out to be the PickMe's of the world. They go hard trying to justify the bullshit they put up with as it pertains to these types of men.

But let me say this really quick, there is absolutely *nothing* wrong with breathing life into your man. However, there is a thin line between being supportive of someone and "building" someone. When you are supportive of a man, he is already established to some degree, he has a vision, a goal, a dream, "a thing" that he is doing, and you are there to cheerlead and give him the love and energy he needs to keep going. He may have a good job, and as his woman, you can encourage him to go for that promotion, take that test, climb a little higher, and keep going. He may have a certain skill or talent he isn't utilizing and as his woman you push him to sharpen his skill and start using his talent. He has already planted a seed and just needs some assistance in helping his dream grow even further. You may see something in him he doesn't see in himself, and vice versa, and you should pull it out of him. You should absolutely encourage your man to give up the good and go for the great! You should date or be with a man you believe in! If you don't believe in your man or see greatness in him then what the hell are you with him for? You should date or be with a man who has goals, who has a plan, who has something on his own outside of you to look forward to. You should be with a man who wakes up every day on a mission to chase his dreams down until he catches up to them, and you should have his back as long as he is on his marathon shit and making progress. Why not? *You should be with a man who you respect enough to not just want to get money from but can also get money with!* Don't let that go over your head's ladies! Oh, but when you have to build a boo, he doesn't have a clue on his own which way to go or what to really do. He's looking to you for assistance. You can't respect a man in this position. This is not how it works. He's talking about it but not being about it. He makes excuses and puts minimal effort into achieving his dream. He's stagnant and plateaus. So now you're the one researching for him, giving him suggestions, rubbing him on the back of his dirty white tee constantly whispering hopeful promises into his bum ass ears, praying that he gets a break so you two can be great. You are the one fixing his resume` and pushing him to do basic shit that a grown man should already have done or know how to do. This is how you wind up supporting his wack ass mix tapes while leaving job applications on his flat ass pillow. You wind up taking on his load and struggles when you simply do not have to, plus you have your own life issues to deal with! That is not what support and holding a man down is. *Your job is to uplift Kings not hold down bums.* Be unapologetic in walking away from a man who is not trying to secure his own future because how can he secure the one he is allegedly building with you? I can only suggest that you not waste your time on these types of men who require way too much help and guidance into their own destiny. Women, *especially black women*, you can't afford to put your life on hold and on the line to try and raise somebody's son anymore. You cannot put your sugar and high blood pressure at risk for folks any more. You can't let these men beat you in the head and make you feel as if you need to settle with them because they choose to settle within themselves. Some men are out here looking for company to support their misery. No. We have done enough. Iyanla Vanzant does not diddy bop in her kitten heels every Saturday night on OWN for women to be out here raising grown ass men. Nah, beloved.

You have nothing to lose when you meet a man and you ask him personal questions about where he is professionally and personally in life, and you decide to walk away because it doesn't match what you are looking for. You have a right, especially if you are out here dating at 40 years old and beyond. You don't have time for dreams; you have to deal with reality! You will have folks tell you that it doesn't matter what a person does for a living, and to focus on who the person is inside. That's bullshit. You have a life to build, things to do, places to go. And yes, he's a *nice guy*, but he aint got shit! So now you are supposed to stick by him and build him up from the ground because *he's nice*? Ted Bundy was nice and now 30 bitches is dead because of him! And if you feel, as a woman, the man you met isn't living up to your standards professionally walk away! Who the hell is teaching you to stay in places that don't serve you right? He owes you nothing to walk away from you if you don't have your shit together either, so let's be crystal clear. Require only what you can reciprocate! It's only fair. And after he checks out on paper, don't be impressed by just that, you still have work to do. You must now find out how he was raised, find out about his relationship with his mother, his children(s) mothers, his exes, his sisters. Check out his friends! Who are his closest buddies and what do they represent? How do they act or carry themselves? What do they do for a living? How do they treat women? How do they treat their mates? Find out if he is healed or if he has anything that he needs to be healed from! Do all of this, of course, if you are serious about being in a relationship. Because some men have no idea how to treat a woman. Rap songs raised them, it's *fuck a bitch* all day or even worse, *if she don't ride for me, aka if I can't drag her through the 36 chambers of death, without her complaining, then she ain't worth it.* So now you have (some) women out here trying to prove their worth to a man by allowing him to put her through all of these "tests" to prove how loyal she is. That's not loyalty, that's stupidity. Then, you have a lot of men out here that only date women who they feel they can manipulate and control. These are the weakest ones of them all. They need to be with someone they can get away with murder with. Most men will only stay with a woman they can manipulate. They need to be with someone whose time they can waste and play with. It's so selfish and not cool. But people are going to be people. It's on YOU, baby girl to not let folks play you and waste your time.

I think one thing we need to keep in mind when we meet a man is that he is not a potential husband or even a potential boyfriend. You do know you can just simply date a guy, no strings attached, and if you do not like him you can choose to no longer see him, you do know that, right? The main purpose of dating is to get to know the guy and get a sense of who he is. But when you are single, looking, and wanting you will pick up any old body and try to make the shit work. When you meet a man, you will learn a lot about him based off of how he spends his time outside of you. What is he into? Where does he go? How does he maximize his time? Is he a doer or a talker? What's his hustle? What's his deal? Also, major key alert! If you are looking for something serious, then don't waste your time with someone who isn't! Don't continue dating a guy who told you or *showed* you from day one that he was going to waste your time. They can tell you anything but within a matter of a few short weeks, even days you can tell if he's full of shit or not. It's all about consistency and energy! Don't fall in love with words, it's all about action! You owe it to yourself to gather as much information as you can so you can see past what's across from you at the dinner table and far beyond what he is telling you. You don't owe him sex or a relationship because he spent money to get to know you over drinks and food. You date to find out what you like, you shop around for a bit, you try shoes on, and you put them back if they don't fit right. That's dating. Let's not complicate things by taking things too far, getting too serious, too fast, or overthinking the situation. Don't let somebody's dusty son sell you a dream and have you stuck in a draining, unproductive relationship. There is nothing worse than being with an emotionally draining man. This man is not on his job. He is not where he wants to be in life, he blames everyone but himself, he leans on you for everything, he has an excuse for everything, and his wage doesn't match his age. Why do we even feel the least bit obligated to attach ourselves to someone who is detached from themselves? Who taught us that we should be attracted to struggle and dysfunction? Who taught us that if it's not a struggle love then it's not real? Who taught us that it was our job to fix broken men? Why is it our problem and our job to come into a man's life to help raise him, fix him, and escort him into a better way of thinking or being, all in exchange for our mental and emotional depletion while we get a dumb ass gold star, complete with a long ass bullshit paragraph on social media, telling all of his followers how we held it down, we a real one, (aka you allowed him to fuck up for years while he figured his life out) complete with a "you my rida" hashtag? Shittin' me! I'm not sure, but we are about to unteach ourselves these dangerous ideas. Because there is no excuse! There are men that I personally know that have done 20 years behind bars, came home, got their master's degree, started businesses, living WELL. And you're out here talking some ol' bullshit? Tell your story walking jack, I don't want to hear it. I'm not interested. Tupac cares, if don't nobody else care though.

Imagine this, imagine a man *loving himself* so much that he doesn't introduce you to struggle, he gets all his affairs in order, mentally, emotionally, spiritually, and financially before stepping out into the world in search of a relationship. Imagine that! Imagine a man so selfless that he would rather let you go then bring you into a world of chaos. Imagine that! Imagine a man that would rather spend time getting himself together than spending time trying to convince you why you should help him get himself together, otherwise you're trash for not riding and dying for him. Because just like when you finally raise a child and you nurture them and give them the tools to succeed they will feel the *natural need* to leave your nest, so they can exercise and execute what they learned in the real world, *elsewhere*. (Most) men will do the same. That is why after (some) women put in all the hard work and dedication building a man up, he shares what he learned with someone else. He leaves you unregrettably and goes on to give the next woman everything you taught him. No man will feel indebted to you because of you holding him down. That shit is bullshit! You do not have to settle for struggle love to be happy. That is not the prerequisite to happily ever after. Step away from men who "need" you in that way. It's toxic, it's unhealthy and it's not fair. It's "**men**ipulation" at its finest! Dating is supposed to be fun! And if it isn't, then you are twerking for the wrong one! You are not the fixer. And he is not your fixer. It is not your job to make him happy, and it is not his job to make you happy. You don't know what demons or skeletons he has, don't go interrupting his karma, leave him be if he's stagnant and unhappy. Trust me, there is nothing you can do. That's an inside job! Run home and burn some sage and "nyamyohorenkyenkyo" your ass back to the positive side of things.

Now, let's get this straight, it's not all about just dating stable men. Make it a point to socialize and become friends with these men as well. It's not just about intimate relationships but healthy platonic ones also. How refreshing does it feel to interact with men who have healthy perspectives and standards as it pertains to women and relationships? Do you have those kinds of conversations with men? What are the men around you telling you about life and love? What are their views on infidelity and family? You do know that you don't have to sit around men, ingesting their derogatory stories and attitudes toward women. Friends or not, you should be around men that value women and want the best for you, so they offer you quality advice. You need positive examples of love and masculinity. Don't absorb the bullshit, sis. Stay in the light! Stay away from toxic masculinity and emotionally unavailable men who walk around playing the victim. Stay away from men who live by the Potential Principle, always talking about what they are *trying* to do or *about* to do or *used* to do. Stay away from conversations and men who want to force feed you the bullshit about all men cheating. There are good men out there, there are faithful men out there, and there are men out there praying for a woman like you! Listen sis, you don't have time to coddle or be there for a man that's not even there for himself. I don't care how cute or fine he is or how good that dick is, that shit gets tired after a short time. You can't love, grow, lean on, or most importantly, learn from a man who isn't productive in his own life. You are to be his helpmate not his doormat. Don't fall for the banana in the tailpipe! You don't have to ride or die for no damn body but yourself! I am convinced that these kinds of men who try to brainwash women to "take care of them and ride with them" were sent by Satan himself to destroy all beautiful and happy things. You don't need to be with a man whose happiness depends on you. If he wasn't happy when you met him, chances are he won't ever be happy. You are not the cure, no matter how dope you are. Get out while you can. Your mental and emotional health depends on it. You need to date someone and be with someone that is also good for your mind and mental health.

We must make better decisions. We must be clear about what we want. We must step out knowing what we deserve and want from a man. You know what you need sis? You need a real ass ni**a. Do you even know what a real ass enword is? Let me tell you what a real ass enword is. A real ass enword is a man that is already a man. *Already a man already*. There is nothing written, documented, or notarized that states that as women, it is our job to raise a man and stick by his side until he gets himself together. And this isn't just about money. This is about dating men who have already done the work and healed from their childhood traumas, men that already have their foot in the door of success and are already well on their way or have arrived and are ready to do the damn thing all over again, men who know their strengths and weaknesses, men that know how to communicate, debate, and listen. Men who have nothing to prove, men who know they are men and command respect by how they carry themselves; therefore, they will treat you right and attract your inner light. Men who aren't caught up in the hype and feel validated by how many women they can lay down. Grown ass men, that are mentally, emotionally, and spiritually ready for a meaningful relationship. Men who respect themselves. Men who have been there, done that, and want no parts of the bullshit. Men who keep you on your toes as a woman because he is a man's man and he's not having any janky shit. Men who are ready to teach, ready to provide, ready to love, nurture, and take care of your entire being. Men who are already men. Men who are already men. Men who are already men already. They did the work, they healed from the trauma, they understood who they were, and who they have become. They are okay with what is. Men who aren't looking for healers, but looking for life partners, someone to share their life with, share their education and success with, share their self-love with, share their home with. Men that want to put you on and see you win. Healthy men. Men you feel good being around, men who make you smile inside. Men who value your time. Men who open doors for you and pull-out chairs. Men who allow you to be free because they don't judge you, they don't try to change you, and they don't compare you to anyone else because you are enough. Men who don't have to try and make you feel inadequate because of their insecurities. Men who support your breath and lift you higher. Men who study you so they can anticipate your needs, men who asks you the important questions about your past, your childhood trauma not to throw it in your face, not to manipulate you or ridicule you but to learn those misunderstood parts about you. Men who allow you to heal all over again with his aide and understanding. Men with empathy, men who understand, men that are human. Men who are at peace with themselves. Solid. Men that are already men. A man that knows how this shit goes, he knows how to treat and speak to a woman with his actions. He knows that intimacy can exist without sex. Men who are complete, men who are already men. Men who are transparent, honest, real, and safe. I don't know about you, but I can't be with someone who I do not feel safe with. I won't vibe well with a man who I don't instantly pick up that vibe with. Because it is indeed an instant feeling you get when you are in that man's presence. And for me, that is what will draw me to a man. And if he isn't healed on top of everything else then he probably won't be loving and affectionate, he will need it more than he can give it. And of course men deserve love and affection just as much as a woman, but if brother ain't healed he ain't loving on nothing but himself. And in turn you will be love starved. How is that fair to you? You deserve a forever love, a man that prepares himself for when he finds you, a man who wants to grow old with you, grow with you, teach you, learn from you, be proud of you, and want what's best for you. A man that worships you, sweats you, adores you, can't keep his hands off of you. A man that's not afraid to show you how much he loves and cares about you. That's a real ass enword. That is what you should be aiming for, that is what you deserve, nothing less. The dusty sons of the world had enough of your time and love. Away with them, off with their heads! But you can't receive or ask for what you can't reciprocate. So make sure you are a woman that is already a woman. A lot of us women pretend to be healed or hide our trauma with superficial things. But the moment of truth always reveals itself when we are angry or scared.

We lash out when we feel as if our past is coming back to haunt us. We are like tea bags, we show our true colors when we are in hot water. We realize it when we begin to feel abandoned or lonely. We get triggered. That means you are not at peace, sis. I want you to be at peace. Work on that so that you can become a better you, and you can attract all the wonderful blessings this world has to offer. We must learn to be at perfect peace with ourselves before we run out there demanding that men already be men when they meet us. It's only fair. If we don't want a build-a-boo then we can't be out here acting like broken birds. We must heal ourselves and be at perfect peace inside. **Peace does not mean perfection.** Perfect peace means that no matter the circumstances surrounding you, your core can't be cracked. You understand the ups and downs of life. You know that disappointment will come but so will attainment. You understand the cycle of life and you're okay with it, you steadily focus inward on your inner joy and peace. When you have peace within, you will stress less, and you won't hold onto anything that doesn't serve you past its statute of limitations. You don't cut people off, you release them, you don't stay angry, you process, and then you let it go. When you have peace inside, you're not easily offended by someone's actions, you find a full understanding instead of demanding a full explanation. So sis, make sure you can reciprocate what you require while you're out there taking applications. Because being at peace means you have arrived at a place in your life where war and tension cannot exist, under any circumstances. Peace means healed. So stay away from those build-a-boo "I need a rider" types. They are not at peace, with their 2 and a possible having asses, meaning they are not good partners, you will not win with him because those types are not healed, they are not healthy to be around. Their only mission is to get a woman that will ride through the pits of hell and back for them. Nah. That ain't love. That ain't about shit. These struggle-men love trying to manipulate the masses into supporting their derelict asses, calling women a 'real one' for being there with them through fuckery. There's no reward for being a real one, just scars. Two things that you need to ask and have clarification on when you are a grown woman out here dating in hopes of settling down. The first thing is, is he healed, and the second thing is, is he free to love me. Being free to love you means there's nobody on this earth that can come to you as a woman. There isn't one woman on this earth that thinks she is in a relationship with him. He is free to love you or anyone that he chooses because he doesn't have any emotional hang ups with himself or anyone else and the only way a man can be free to love a woman and give her his all is if he is healed from anything in his past that once hurt or hindered him. Find out if your dude is healed and free sis. I'm not sure if someone is reading this right now knowing that they are dealing with someone that is emotionally draining, unfocused, and lazy. I'm not sure if someone is reading this and feeling a way because the man, they are with is an underperformer, and they know it deep in their hearts, but they just *see something in him* so they can't let him go or perhaps they don't want to feel the guilt of turning their back on him while he is "trying." Perhaps they feel guilty for doing better than him. All I can tell you is a grown man who doesn't have anything to show for the years he's been on this earth doesn't plan on showing you a damn thing. Cut your losses. This ain't it, chief. Flick your cigarette at that enword and say it in honor of the leader of Black Don't *Ever* Crack, Angela Bassett in Waiting to Exhale: *It is trash.*

I think for us to have healthy relationships we must start being honest with one another. We must communicate better. We must be okay with being transparent and expressing ourselves. He/she can't love you the way you deserve if you're lying about who you are. They are going to wind up loving the representative and not the real you. Relationships don't have to be so struggly and hard. Get you a real ass ni**a, a hustler, not to be confused with a drug dealer but a hustler. He is going to go out there and get it for himself and his loved ones. And even if he doesn't have it all, his motivation and drive to go get it is enough to make you want to ride with him. You have no idea how much you can uplift a man and how far he can go and take the relationship when you come to the table with confidence, consistency, authenticity, no Pick Me shit, no struggle vibes, just like how you want your man to be. If two people are being honest out the gate and truly accepting of one another, relationships could be so beautiful. As long as that respect is there, even when it ends, it doesn't have to end in pain and anger. You have to stop hiding your demons and putting them on other people. It's time to be real with yourself and real with whom you share space with. You have to love yourself enough and be confident enough in yourself to bear all and allow people to choose to love you for who you are or walk away for that very reason. You gotta just deal with it and not manipulate folks. That mask is gonna fall sooner or later. Why waste your time and someone else's? Just be you! You are enough! And the right person will grow with you and love on you regardless. And you will respect and love on that brother no matter how flawed he is because you know where he is coming from. That's love, respect, that's a relationship... that's a real ass ni**a.

The moral of the story is this:

You date at the level of your esteem. Keep that in mind the next time you look at your lover and feel disgust.

Message!

There is nothing wrong with standards. In fact, I think men find it attractive when women have standards, and they only pass you over when they aren't ready to settle down. Keep your standards. You gotta test these men to make sure he is who he says he is. So take your time, feel him out and if he's a solid man of his word and he's consistent, that's when you go all out. That's when you hold him down, build him up, ride with him and have his back because he is going to do the same for you. That's what a solid man does. He doesn't put the weight on you to carry things, as proof of you being a real one or a down ass bitch, nah. A solid man would never! He is already standing tall. You merely showed up and made him want to be *even better* because of the kind of woman that YOU are. He knows to keep you he has to remain on his A-game. And you also know that you are in the presence of a good man, so you need to be on your A-game as well. One hand washes the other. You need a man that you can be proud of, a man that you see greatness in and want to help elevate. His back might be a little crooked, that's cool, help him stand a little taller! He has to see the same in you! His heart will swell with pride when he looks at you, because you are a woman's woman, and you didn't come in and save him nor did you need saving. You have to leave a man with his dignity. If you come into a relationship saving him, treating him like a boy then what does he have? It is not your job, that's his parents' job!! Your job is to ride a shotgun with him and keep him company while he does what he needs to do, grab the wheel when he needs a break from driving. Relationships are a partnership. You have to be able to rely on and trust one another in order for it to work. Relationships only prove to be difficult when one of you doesn't want to be in it, therefore you're not going to put in the work that it takes to maintain it. Also, pick a man that has standards as well! Yup, choose someone who takes care of himself, respects himself, and has something to lose. If he has nothing to protect, then he has nothing to offer you. He has to have his own thing going on that he isn't willing to share with just anybody, so when he does choose you, you know its special, and you know he values you because he is bringing you into the space and life that he values and carved out for himself as a man. He's not going to just share where he lives, his emotions, his family, and friends with just anybody because he aint for everybody. This ain't community peen. He got gated community dick. That's the man you want. He's protecting his Kingdom, he's protecting his reputation, and he's not willing to just date any ole woman. He ain't for everybody. And if he chooses you, he's going to protect you too. But make sure you are that kind of woman as well. Have something sacred going on in your life that's not for everybody, but for that special one. You are on the right track girlie, stay solid!

6 PICK MEEEEE BABY!

What is a "Pick Me" you ask? A Pick Me is typically a woman who needs admiration, validation, and attention from men so badly that they play themselves and cater to the egos of men as well as putting themselves on a pedestal while talking shit about how other women "take care" of men. Pick Me women create memes that go viral, telling women how to be, for a man to appreciate them. They stand out amongst "regular" women with their basic relationship survival tactics and ridiculous views on intimate relationships. The Pick Me is not well received by general population because folks don't like when you come off as *better than*. The Pick Me typically makes comments about what a woman needs to do for her man in the presence of men in hopes of being, well you guessed it, picked! She wants to appear to have better morals than all the other women. Pick Meez often find themselves going through lots of changes because a Pick Me is a fictional character to begin with. Pick Me women aren't real people, they are made up characters put on earth to annoy the fuck out of everyone that's comfortable in their own skin. The Pick Me will go through a lot of changes trying to fit in. Instead of finding some relaxation they attack everybody who seems to be having fun. Pick Meez are the fun police. Pick Me women always wind up twerking for the wrong enword because they are relentless when it comes to thinking that their basic wife skills will change a man and make him want to settle down. She feels as if she is such a *good woman*, that any man would be lucky to have her. I mean after all, she doesn't do clubs, she doesn't go out, she doesn't smoke or drink, her dream job is to just take care of her man and agree with everything that he says because on top of everything else, sis is his peace too. The Pick Meez end game is to be perceived as a good girl, a good woman, and to be chosen for her great qualities that no other woman possesses. She is the reigning unproblematic Queen of the Universe. She doesn't twerk and she doesn't say no to *anything* that her man asks of her. She stays home so that he will know without a shadow of a doubt that she isn't *out there* like those *other bitches.*

Well guess what, if there are any Pick Meez or potential Pick Meez reading this, listen up. The enword that you're trying to impress with this basic ass shit is *out there*, where you ask? With the "other bitches" that you so desperately want to separate yourself from. He is out there communicating with HUMANS, you hear me? HUMANS! Your behavior is that of a fucking lifeless robot. So he is out there interacting with folks who have actual heart beats and has other things to do other than wait on him hand and foot. But let you tell it, these women are trash, beneath you, *unworthy.* They need to be home preparing a meal for their King and serving him pussy on a platter. No, actually sis, those women are living their best life and not sitting around waiting for some man to make them feel worthy or give them a gold star for doing basic ass woman shit. Listen, I hate to break the news to you Pick Meez, but you're not the only one with a pot and a throat sis. Go outside, he gon cheat anyway. You can stay home, suck him, fuck him, help him start a business, have his kids and even marry his ass. But baby, gonna need to start a Go Fund Me for a new set of legs bitch because you are not gonna be able to stand it when he leaves your ass for the love of his life. And she's not gonna have to do a fraction of shit that you're doing to

"make him happy." You are doing all of this for nothing. But the Pick Me won't give up, she is going to change this man with her good girl magical powers and her super pussy that works around the clock for her man to help himself to whenever he wants it! She is going to lure him away from Thotville because everyone outside of her are thots, right? She's going to fly in and swoop him up and bring him into a world of normalcy and perfection. She is going to keep him happy by sweeping around his feet, rubbing his balls, while cooking Sunday dinner because she does all things, and she is every woman and no task is too big or too

Twerkin And The City

small for the Pick Me. She wouldn't dare tell her man no, no matter how tired she is and risk another woman doing it for him? You got her fucked up. She's not taking a chance. You know how this story ends right? The Pick Me winds up getting used for all her resources, ran all over, left, cheated on or all of the above. And then will come with the rant of:

I did everything for him! I cooked, I cleaned, I never said no to sex, I was always home, I didn't give him any problems, I gave him money, I stayed out of his way when he was in a bad mood, I was his ride or die, I was good to him!

Ah! But did he ask you to do all that? Yeah, it sounds cold but it's real. Did he ask you? You did all those things to make yourself feel good and to outdo any other female that he might possibly have his eye on or might have an eye on him. Who told you it made him feel good? You asked why he would cheat on you after all you did for him. Well, ask yourself if the things you did for him actually made him happy? Sometimes less is more Ms. Pick Me, that's all I'm saying. Not to mention, all those jabs that you throw at other women all day, putting them down for not being you is wack and a turn off and though most men won't say anything, they take notes, they get turned off, and they inevitably run right into the arms of the kind of woman you are trying to deter them from. There is nothing sexy about downing other people to your man. It reeks of insecurity. It's not cool. If you are confident in who you are then you don't have to talk shit about anybody for that matter. Just do you!

In the Pick Meez's defense, I do think that they strategically act this way because we are living in an era of Hot girls, Thots, Winning Hoes, and women out here period just not giving a fuck about anybody's opinions. Shout out to the City Girls and Meg the Stallions of the world who are out here doing what the hell they want to do! But regular day to day women are out here living as well, baby! We are out here free'er, flier, and better than we have ever been, so ain't nobody fittna use this time foolishly by sheltering themselves in any way fathomable. So the Pick Meez probably feel that they will stand out by being the opposite of what society is attracted to. I mean I get it, why try to fit in when you can stand out, right? But see, this is how you wind up in the wrong enwords's face, trying too hard to be different to stand out. You are going to attract a man that wants nothing more than to prove to you that it doesn't matter what you do, his choice and his preferences are his and you can't do anything to change that. Yet you rather date the opposite of what you know is right for you to prove a point. I could be wrong but all the Pick Meez I have encountered want to be like the women they slander, and they go after the attention of men that they know damn well are out of their league in some kind of way. Pick Meez, I want to give you a word of advice. Stop settling and selling yourself short. You don't have to play meek to get a man to respect you or be with you. Stop doing the most to be chosen and start doing the choosing! You want to be his peace and his parole officer, his woman and his homeboy, his wife and his boss, his breath and his lungs, his dick and his balls, my goodness get a grip! Pick Meez are always selling themselves short just to appear unproblematic to these enwords. For example, Pick Meez will say something like:

> *"We don't have to go out, it doesn't make sense to spend money on a date at a restaurant when we can just order pizza. We can even just sit in your car and talk, your time is more valuable."*

Now sis. Come on, we are grown women here. You know good and damn well you want to throw on a sexy cocktail dress and be shown off, as you should! Why be so humble? The bible didn't teach you that, did it? The bible doesn't say be humble, it says to humble yourself and that's on a case-by-case basis and when you are dating that is not the time to humble yourself, that is the time to big up yourself and be treated in a way you deserve! Because beloved, while he is feeding you pizza with your humble ass, another woman is out there dabbing her mouth with a soft linen napkin, in preparation for entree number 3 at Tao's, but go on and be basic if you think that's the way to a man's heart. Sheesh, at least request a date to a bottomless brunch or something, damn. Spare no man's pockets. If he's old enough to fuck, he's old enough to spend. Pick Meez will also preach that you should cook and clean for your man, give him sex when he wants it, and do your own nails and hair because why have him pay for it, he's not an ATM, he's a man! Fuck outta here. Have his back even when he's wrong, allow him to cheat because he is a man and men make mistakes, take care of him, build your King, stand by him through thick and thin if you're a *real woman*. You know what? You are right. Allow him to make mistakes, raise him up, show him the way, teach him, and be his peace. Do all things through Christ who strengthens him. Go right ahead. And while you're at it, claim him on your taxes since you want a son so fucking bad. This ain't it, Pick Me! You don't have to build-a-boo or build a man up just to prove you are worthy of his love! You do know that there are some *fully assembled* enwords running around here, right? Batteries included and all! Yet, you refuse to get one. Your validation comes from finding these broken down enwords and building them, for what? I don't know, remember I told yawl I don't know shit, so don't hold my words against me. I'm trying to figure this whole thing out as well. But one thing I do know for sure is that, being a Pick Me ain't the way. If you would just stop running, jumping, and diving into these men's central vision and stop trying to get picked by putting other women down and just do you, you will turn out just fine.

Pick Meez will play up their own haves while downing the have nots. Sis, he doesn't care that you own your home and the woman you think he's attracted to lives in an apartment. Sis, he doesn't care that you have degrees, and the other girls have GED's, sis he does not care that you don't drink, and the other woman gets 4 loko wasted on Tuesday nights. Sis, he does not care, not one iota of a fuck about your body count and how many "serious" relationships you've been in versus ole girl that be pussy poppin on a handstand, on her lunch break, much to the dismay of her coworkers at the nursing home. I'm not sure if anyone reading this will admit that they are guilty of downing other women to big themselves up but just know that it's unnecessary. We are all beautiful and worthy of love. Maybe you can learn something from women that don't share your beliefs such as they can learn from you. At the end of the day, all you are doing is showing everyone how insecure you are and how envious you are of other women that have the courage to be who they really are. Let other people be great and focus on just being yourself! You're fucking perfect for someone who wants everything that you have to offer even if you are annoying as hell, and you won't have to shit on other women or do the most to get him! Someone wants your basic chicken alfredo, baby girl. No need to shade what someone else has going on in their kitchen.

The moral of the story is this:

Your man thinks your annoying and talks shit about you behind your back. But ya credit is banging and you don't ask him for money towards the rent so he's staying and stacking. But once he reaches his financial goal, your days are numbered sis.

Message!

I'm aware that I may possibly have some young readers, so I want to address my beautiful Princesses. Life is about lessons indeed. But you don't have to live a life of hard times, bad decisions, and painful memories, young Queen. Right now you are growing up in an era that is very dangerous and toxic. The agenda being forced on you goes against everything that a respectful young woman should be. Right now you are made to believe that the only way to make it is to be promiscuous, get paid to show your body, spend an obscene amount of money on hair weave and make up, and scam/steal to get designer things so that you can fit in with the *in crowd*. Right now you are made to believe that your sexuality is what will get you to the top. You are made to believe that the body God gave you is not good enough and that you should alter it with surgery. Nowhere in this world are you taught to love yourself for who you are. Your mother is only 16 years older than you. She wants you to be her friend so she can't really guide you from an adult's perspective. Your father is in jail or in the streets on his way to jail, but in the meantime the studio is his bitch but he will make time for you when a photo-op comes along for IG. #Daddysgirl. Your parent(s) may be hard workers and unfortunately can't give you the time you require because they have to keep food on the table. Don't despise them, they are doing the best that they can. Life is hard sometimes. Right now your only job is to be good to yourself and not get caught up in the race of trying to keep up with the joneses. You are thinking of or actually doing things that doesn't compliment your true self. Young girl, if nobody tells you, let me be the first to say that you don't have to try to fit in. Don't follow the crowd, they are lost as fuck. You are too young to contemplate surgery. Your body hasn't gone through anything that you can't work out in the gym. Give yourself time to grow. Get to learn yourself. Don't let rap lyrics raise you. Don't perpetuate a hard life for sympathy just to try and fit in with the truly lost souls that don't stand a chance. No matter your circumstances you are young. You have time to rebuild your life and do things differently than what you see and what you are being taught. These young boys truly only want one thing from you and that is to conquer you. They want to play house and grown-up on your time. They want to have sex with you then tell their friends about how open they got you. They want to run through every girl in the world. You, my dear, are not special to any young boy. Young boys have no idea what they want out of life. You are merely a bridge they will walk over and cross back over time and time again until you eventually break. You don't have to look back over your life and reminisce over hard times. You don't have to have a hard life if you make wise decisions about who your friends are, who you give your body to, what you spend your idle time doing, and how much energy and effort you put into securing your reputation and character as a young lady.

Right now you are being forced to believe that being in a relationship validates you. #RelationshipGoals. And it's possible that your home isn't the happiest, so you might be out there looking for love. Relationships are not just cute pictures of a boy and a girl dressed in the same colors, kissing each other. Relationships are hard work, hard work that you are too young to be entertaining. Babygirl, you will find that everything you are looking for is right inside of you and no boy in this world can give you self-love. Do not step out into this world young, vulnerable, and needy. The wolves will eat your ass up! Stay in your lane, grow, and love on yourself as hard as you can. Fight the urge to become dependent on the compliments and company of others. Your solitude is your power. As long as you can enjoy being alone with your own company, you will do just fine. You have all the time in the world to date, to be a grown-up and to do adult things. You will be older way longer than you will be younger so enjoy the years of going to school, picking out colleges, living at home, saving your money, and being free from the world without true adult responsibilities and emotions. Sit back and enjoy your youth. Observe everyone around you. They're not as happy as they pretend to be. It's not all Fashion Nova and bundles, baby. These girls need love and attention and will do whatever they have to do to get it. You, my dear, are different. You have someone telling you that you don't have to do all that. Just focus on yourself and be the best you can be without the validation of others. Your opinion of you is all that matters. Chin up! Grades high! Self-Love on fleek!

7 …. BUT SHE AINT MESSING WITH NO BROKE NI**A

*Birdman Hand Rub** Let me set the tone for this chapter right here and right now. You are a grown woman with a sophisticated palate. You should not under *any circumstances* be out here arguing with somebody's dusty ass son, about how much he is going to spend on a date. *Period.*

Now, anytime there is a discussion about money, temperatures rise. The debates get out of control. It's like a spades game in a black household on a Saturday night! I cannot believe that it has come to this, we are now debating and beefing on how much a date should cost. In 2019, "men" are out right telling women if they spend $200 on a date, that they deserve some pu**y from them. Okay I'm getting ahead of myself. Let's talk about "gold diggers" first. I have this conversation with men often, and I always get two sides to this hot topic. On one hand, I have men say that the reason why a lot of women are single is because they want to *get paid* to be in a relationship, meaning that a woman isn't willing to be with a man unless he is *"financially generous."* Then on the other hand, I have had conversations with men who have said a woman is foolish to deal with a man, *especially sexually,* that doesn't spend money on her. Ironically enough, the men I have talked to *that have money* are the ones that suggest that a woman should be taken care of and the ones that don't have any gold for a woman to dig for are the ones to suggest that women should not make money a factor in whether they will date a person. While I take both sides into consideration, let me say this: I feel no shame in saying with 100% confidence that I will only date someone that will treat me the way I treat myself. I enjoy nice things, I provide myself with nice memories, trips, dining experiences, etc., and so I do expect a mate that will keep that same energy with me when I let him into my life. I never ask for more than I deserve. I am by no means a Gold Digger but I ain't messing with no broke ni**a. It costs to date a grown woman. *The courtroom erupts, the judge bangs her gavel* Order! Order!

Let me explain something to you about men and *gold diggers*. First things first, wanting the presence and confirmation of a man's finances doesn't mean the absence of a woman's own! Financially challenged men think that any woman who wants to eat at a nice restaurant is a gold digger because they cannot afford to give her the 5-star experience, at least not consistently if at all. Look don't come for me. Jay Z is the one that said if you can't buy it twice then you can't afford it. But the way a man feels about a so-called gold digger is his own insecurities, not the woman! That's my observation. They attempt to make a woman feel as if she is asking for too much or her wants are unrealistic. The moment a man is able to do any and everything for a woman, the first thing they do is snatch up a woman and splurge. Same broke man yesterday hating on gold diggers is the same man that would wife one if he hit the mega millions. In summation, there is no such thing as a gold digger. A gold digger is

what a man calls women that he wants but can't afford, that's all. She's not a gold digger, she's a grown woman that knows what she likes and dates that type. She's not about to go back and forth with you enwords about how much her meal should cost, especially if she can afford to do it herself! Are you dumb? And for fucks sake why is it that any other race of women in the world can go after men with money but black women are called Gold Diggers when we do it? A grown woman that takes care of herself, respects herself, provides the best for herself to the best of her ability, and wants to date men that treat themselves with that same integrity as well as wanting to treat her that way, is not a gold digger! Other races groom and raise their daughters to go after a man that can provide for them financially and nobody bats an eye. But

let a sista get her a good man worth a few dollars, folks want to bring
up her past, talk shit about her, accuse her

of being in it for the money. It's disgusting. Who doesn't love money? Who doesn't want to live well? What adult woman that you know, would want to date a man that isn't taking care of himself, therefore there is no way that he can take care of her? What mother would not instruct her daughter to be with someone that will be able to take care of her? Wanting a man that can take care of a woman does not mean the absence of a woman's own financial independence, let's be clear. Why are we left to feel as if we should not be attracted to or desire a man with money but everybody else can? So then what some women do is *settle* to prove that *"she isn't like that"* Nah, fuck that, we are like that! And we deserve it. Go get your money sis! Another thing that leaves me befuddled is that there are men that will flaunt their riches then start crying when a woman expects to be taken care of. What are you flashing for if you don't want a woman to have some of it? Aren't you flashing so you can attract women? Aren't you sending out the signal that you have money, come and get it? No, okay well make sure that you keep that same energy when you see a woman dressed in skimpy clothes. Don't assume she wants you to rape her or make vile passes at her just because of the way she is dressed. So what is it, you want to lure women in just to deny them access to your material bullshit? Even worse is when men expect you to put up with some fuckery to prove you are *worthy* of being taken out to eat at a nice restaurant. Only fuck boys play those games and only needy bitches will play along and they deserve one another. But grown women won't waste not one second on somebody's dusty son complaining about the cost of a date and lucky for grown women, grown men don't have time for that, so go get you one. Anthony Hamilton did not sing the slaves to freedom for grown twomen to be out here accepting BBQ's as a date or to be out here waiting on some man to treat them nice.

No grown woman *that I know is* walking into something new with a man that doesn't have himself together and that can't provide the basics such as consistent quality dates. Every date doesn't have to be expensive, but it definitely has to be of **quality.** If the man is showing you interest and wants to be around, you then he has to come up with ways to keep you entertained and it's going to cost. Even his time is costly so if he doesn't plan on spending a lot of money on a date then he must be one hell of a talker and charmer to distract you from the fact that yawl ain't doing much of anything. We don't have anything to prove by staying with a man that turns us off because he doesn't know how to date like an adult, and the reason being because his money is jacked up or because he feels it's a waste of money, and he can do something else with his $200. There's a whole colony of Pick Meez somewhere for that, bro. Grown women want to go out and eat quality food and if you don't agree, that's cool, skip this chapter and don't debate me, debate that cold ass pizza he left in your fridge from the previous chapter. The rest of you read along because at the end of the day, it is my belief and understanding that you're supposed to give a bum spare change, not pussy, but whatever. What do I know? I'm single, maybe because my standards are too high. But I work hard, so why can't I get a good meal without complaints?

Let me ride in this lane real quick and talk to you about a bum and a broke Enword. Being a bum is a mentality. I know some rich bums. They're mentally and morally poor. All they have is money. Money makes them. Money makes them treat people a certain way. They look down on people. They wake up every day just to taunt and stunt on people with less than them. Those are bums. If they lost it all today, they would have nothing. Not a friend to help them or means to get it back, because they are bums inside. And then there's the *real bums.* They don't want shit. They are ok with living in poverty or in mediocrity. They have no goals. They're not ambitious about anything. They just find people to latch on to so that they can manipulate them into taking care of them. BUMS! And you shouldn't give any of these men your time or your lady parts. But hey! It's your pussy, so your rules. Then you have these broke men. I'm not talking about the hard-working men in the world who just so happen to not be millionaires. Every man isn't a baller. That does not make him broke or a bum! There are some good ass hard working men out there bringing in good salaries that knows how to budget and spend money accordingly. They live good, drive nice cars, eat, and dress well. They don't just throw money away because they work too hard for it! So if this man chooses to not spend money on you, it's not because he's some broke ass ni**a, it's possible that he isn't really checking for you like that, at least not right now, so he's not going all out like that! He would like to know where his money is going before he starts treating you like wifey. Just relax sis. But then you got a broke ass ni**a that has a good job, and he blows it on Henny and Hookahs. He's unkempt, he doesn't take care of himself. You go to his crib and its sneaker boxes and liquor bottles everywhere. He doesn't have any class. He doesn't know what a quality date is. He ain't never been nowhere and he ain't tryna go nowhere. That's broke ni**a shit. I just wanted to clear that up. Shout out to the good men, the hard-working blue collar 9-5 men. Any man that is out there working hard, not asking for handouts, providing for himself, and doing what he has to do is alright with me. You're a boss in my eyes baby.

Additionally, it's easy for a man that "got it" to give it to you. But when a man that's not a baller goes out of his way to try and please you, that is something you should not take for granted. Having money doesn't make him a real one, having a heart and being kind and generous to you is what makes him a real one. You want to be exclusive to any man you deal with, not be treated, and tossed bread at like one of the little chickens in his pigeon coop.

Men get so offended sometimes over this whole cost of dating thing, and I don't know why. If you don't want to spend over a certain amount on dates, just don't! Why go so hard trying to bash the women that have an issue with cheap dates? Let them date who they want, and you date who you want. But see the men that bash women who like quality dates are mad because those are the kind of women they want but can't have. Women are not suggesting you bust up your paycheck on restaurants. But it says a lot about a man when the first thing he does is complain about the cost of a date. It's a turn off and a major red flag. Women don't need to hear men complaining about money, not early in the game...not never. Honestly, the last thing that any man *or woman* should be doing, if their finances aren't in order, is dating. A (grown) woman wants security and stability and if you are complaining about feeding her, what message are you sending? She's not sticking around! Is that a crime? Yes, we want you to have what it takes to provide a good life for us, *and*? Where's the crime? Why are men trying to make us feel as if this is a bad thing? We want to be treated nicely.

Where is the crime? You know what else a grown woman wants and requires? We require you to have your own place and gainful employment, at the very least, and have them 401k accounts and pensions in place. Grown women are not out here fucking for bags and shoes. Grown women want Pension Penis and Retirement Funds Fellatio. We want forever dough, not flash now, but time will reveal money. And grown women have no problem contributing to this good life as well! Grown women are not asking you to go at it alone! But we will be damned if we are pulling the bulk of the load and there is a whole grown ass man calling himself our man. Grown women aren't *pressed* over the cost of no punk ass dinner dates, cuz.

All this talk about expensive dates is just for debate but grown women want to know about future plans not dinner plans. **#Barz**. And lastly, yes, we want you to be financially straight for the obvious. How are you going to court a grown woman if you're broke? So, you think the woman is going to pay for everything? Let's be real, women love money, we love to be taken out, we love going on vacation, we love gifts and there is no need to apologize or pretend we don't just so somebody's dusty ass son doesn't feel inadequate! This is how you wind up twerkin for the wrong enword, when you dumb yourself down to make him feel good. Men won't ever deny loving pussy will they? And that's okay too. But can we all just be honest and admit that outside of what you really need in a relationship (*love, attention, communication, respect, yes the obviously important stuff*); additionally, most if not all, women want a man that "got it?" If Receiving Gifts is one of your love languages, then stand in your truth and don't let some fool with a 450-credit score make you feel bad about that. Speaking of love languages, do you know what your love language is and what your lover's love language is? Ah! Now that is the important question! There are 5 love languages provided by Gary Chapman: **Words of Affirmation,**

Acts of Service, Receiving Gifts, Quality Time, and

Physical Touch. I think once you are aware of your love language and your lover's love language then you can have a better understanding of what the give and take in the relationship will be. I'm a Physical Touch, Quality Time, Receiving Gifts woman. I need my man to touch me subtly for no reason at all. Place your big ole hand on my thigh, rest your hands in the dip of my lower back while we are walking, kiss my shoulder, hug me. I need you to make time for me definitely. Don't squeeze me in but come see about me when I know you could be sleep after working so hard. Show me I'm special by the time you put in. I need that time fellas! I need that consistency. I need to know and feel without a doubt that I am your woman. Of the three, if I had to choose it would be quality time. And yes, I love receiving gifts be it a night out or actual gifts. No matter how big or small, no matter how much it costs, it is all about **QUALITY**. But that's me, and I know that in order to have those needs fulfilled I have to date a man that respects that and shares the same love languages as me. I'm not going to kid myself and date someone that doesn't respect my love language. For what? When a man makes time for you, it sends the message that he is making you a part of his routine, a part of his day and what's important to him. You are on his to-do list, you are included in the day to day things that he deems important and must take care of before he goes to sleep at night. Anybody can buy you gifts, any man with money can spend it on you, anybody can touch you, but not everyone will carve out a space in their day to spend time with you because they miss you and enjoy being around you. Not only is he making time for you but making time to implement you into his world, his life, and his home. So figure out your love language and be honest with yourself about what means the world to you and date those kinds of people!

But back to this shmoney honey. No matter the love language, women love to be able to *feel free* when they are around a man. We want to feel as if *"he got this."* No, we don't want to go dutch. We don't want to worry about if you can afford the meal. Women want a man that got it! Period! We don't want to be concerned with a bill or none of that, not while we are dating. We don't want to feel as if we can't order what we want because he may expect something at the end of the night. We don't want to be anywhere near that kind of energy or pressure. Come on now ladies, don't leave me hanging! We want a man we can be honest with when he asks us where we want to eat. We don't want to act like we don't know because we aren't sure of your budget. Ladies, isn't that one of the main reasons why we are so indecisive when asked where do we want to eat? Fellas, it's because most of the time we don't know your budget! See, we're not gold diggers, we take your feelings into consideration, and you don't even appreciate it. We know damn well we want to eat at Brooklyn Chop House tonight, but we won't say it unless we know for sure you won't have an issue, so we'll leave it up to you and pray you can afford it comfortably. But what I'm not doing is having a debate with somebody's dusty ass son about what's too expensive to be spending on a date with me. I'll go by my damn self and leave you home eating General Tso's from the corner store. That conversation will *never* ever happen with me. I am a grown woman, and I personally am not dating a man that's going to argue with me about $200 being too much for a date. And let's be crystal clear. It's not about the cost of the date, it's the nerve of a man wanting to spend time with you, yet he's complaining about what he's *not* going to do for you. No ma'am. I'm not gon' be able to do it!

Sis, look at yourself. Look in the mirror. You deserve every good thing in this world and at the very least you deserve great company and a great damn meal. To those of you reading that may possibly disagree with me, you may be saying to yourself, it's not all about money, let me ask you this: Would you move into a man's home and pay half of his bills because he can't hold his own? Mind you, you are already paying your own rent/mortgage by yourself. Are you willing to move him into your home bill free? Are you cool with going dutch with the man you are seeing? Are you cool with paying for vacations or going half on trips with the man you are laying up with? Are you cool with buying all the groceries after he done came over and ate up everything? Are you cool with your man not having any money? Are you cool with the grown ass man that you are dating not being able to take you out to quality places? Are you cool with him not being able to do for himself because he has clearly been irresponsible all his life and now as a grown man, he has nothing to show for his time on this earth. Are you cool with that? Are you cool with having to dumb down your lifestyle because the man you are dating can't afford to do the things that you like? Oh and might I add, you are doing all of this for yourself already! The vacations, the bills, shows, concerts, the fine dining. You're telling me you're okay with inviting a man into your life that can't match that or upgrade that? You still out here chanting that you can't depend on no enword for shit? Baby girl, maybe it's the men *you're* dealing with that you can't depend on. Listen, back in the day, the man went out, worked, hunted, brought the kill home, and the woman cooked it, finessed it and took care of the house. The man's job was to provide and protect. But before we get to that stage, they are supposed to court us and do whatever they can to get us in their good graces and to build our trust and make us feel as if we can be safe with him. Whose fault is it that men are complaining about spending money on a quality date? Whose fault is it that men don't have the patience to get to know us, and they just want to get in our panties? Who's to blame for this? Somewhere along the line our signals got crossed and roles started switching. There is nothing wrong with being independent. As an adult, yes you have to take care of yourself, ladies. Allow a man to feed you and you give him the power to starve you. So you have to always have your own thing going on. But you also have to fall back and let him treat you like a lady. This whole independent woman thing is blowing mines, honestly. I don't want no parts. LOL. I need my dude to handle his business, be all about his money, all about me, and know that I am official enough to hold us down if things get a little janky. Ladies, your guy must feel as if you can hold shit down too. Don't ever forget that. But these men are out here talking about, fuck a bitch, I'll do for my bros before I do for some bitch. I ain't chasing no bitch. Why not sir!? You better chase that bitch! Who raised these jokersl? Once a man comes into your life and starts taking up your time and laying between your thighs, things change! It is my understanding that men are supposed to court us, protect us, provide for us, and treat us like the beautiful flowers that we are and if he can't keep that same energy while dating, then he shouldn't date because grown women also need consistency, so *"he"* shouldn't start something he can't finish then put pressure on you to settle! Because no matter how well a woman is doing in life, we all want a man that will make us feel as if he got our backs and will do for us regardless. It's not for you to dumb down your wants and needs to please any damn body. Still not clear? Let me put it to you like this:

If you have stamps on your passport and you meet a guy that doesn't like to or can't afford to travel, are you going to stop traveling the world because he can't? It should be a prerequisite that anyone you date has stamps as well, or at the very least be willing to accumulate some and can afford to. Why waste time on someone that's not on the same page as you? But the bottom line is, grown men act like grown men and they don't care about $200 dates and all that nonsense. These dates are an investment into the woman he is attracted to and wants to be with. It's just a quick glimpse into what she can expect should he decide to take the next step. Grown men don't complain about the things that "other" men complain about. They wine and dine without whining and crying. They pay for things, they assist, they provide, they offer help whether the woman needs it or not, whether you're his lady or not, some men are just like that. Being a grown man is a state of mind. They understand that time is money, so even if he's not putting the cash in your hand, the experience within itself will be of quality. It's not about the cost, it's about the experience! He will take you to quality places because just like you, he's into quality things. Grown men aren't taking you to Olive Garden sweetie. Not to say there is anything wrong with that, but if your palate is mature, you more than likely will experience different dining experiences with grown men, it comes with no trivia, and will definitely cost over $200. Grown men feel as if since they are dating you or taking up your time, they are going to make it worth it not just for you but for him as well! Grown men are taking care of the bill and not stressing no pussy out of you just because they spent $200 on a date. That's fuck boy shit.

Men want a million damn things from a woman: head until your jaws lock, good sex, riding dick flat footed for more than 2 minutes, home cooked meals, a freaky virgin, 1 kid or no kids, a flat stomach, a fat ass, long hair, and all this nonsense just to beef about some $200 date? These men today don't even romance women anymore. I get that there are thots and hoes running around that are deemed unworthy of a man's respect, and I get that you can't treat everyone the same, but these men aren't putting in any effort to show a woman they care. They are no longer trying to impress us with chivalry. We can't get head or a quality meal. But they want us to come over, with their thirsty asses and can't even make us cum when we get there. You go to a man's house these days and there's no music playing, just 2k on pause on the flat screen. There are no oils lit, there's nothing good to eat, no ambience, and no mood, just bullshit conversation to kill time before they're trying to stuff their dicks down your throat. Men nowadays have no class but want to always beef about money being spent. They equate having money to having class. I don't care what you got if you ain't spending it on me number one, number two, if your attitude sucks and you have no class, ain't nobody putting up with your bullshit just because you got some change. Grown women do not care about that shit. Cassie did not stay with Diddy for 10 years then left him and found true love with his personal trainer and move on to live happily ever after for us to be out here arguing with nobody's dusty son about how much he thinks we're worth on a date. I'll feed myself first, because listen, I order appetizers and I order from the *"fucking"* side of the menu with no shame or pressure to have sex with a man later. I don't even give the impression that it's a possibility. *Sir,* if we are out having dinner, assuming we go somewhere even half decent, you're looking at roughly $30 a plate. That's already $60 between you and I for dinner. Now before our entrees arrive, do not pump fake and ask me do I want appetizers, because the answer will be yes. *Yes,* I'll have an order of Clams Casino please with an order of calamari, sir. That's about $50 right there. What am I drinking? Grand Marnier, double, neat please. That double is $24 at least, so do the math. You haven't ordered any drinks yet, and I'm just getting started. Do I have class? Yes! Am I ordering mad shit just because it's on your dime? No. This is what I do, whether with friends or men. So I'm not going to dumb down my dining experience because you're uncomfortable. Don't date me then! Ayana is going to eat regardless. Yes, I am going to more than likely have at least 3 rounds of those double Grand Marnier's because life is stressful, I worked hard all week, and I can be in bed resting but I'm out here with you. My tab alone is roughly $200. You now have to worry about *your* tab which will be around the same, providing you don't starve yourself to save money. You might have a service charge on your hand and the tip. Round this bitch out to about $400. I'll pay the tip sir, I'm a lady. If you choose to walk out or go dutch at this point that's cool, I can feed me sir, thanks. That's grown woman stuff and any man that can't respect that doesn't need to waste your time, ladies. Now depending on the kind of man he is, this may or may not be a lot of money. I am not judging any man that isn't willing to spend that on a date. He is entitled! And that's just one example because dates don't cost $400; *however*, on a good night, if you are having fun and don't want to leave one another's presence you may wind up eating, bar hopping, shooting pool, and doing miscellaneous stuff plus cab rides home if nobody drove in and the night may cost you $400, so think about it! And I do not know if his cable is going to get cut off after this date nor do I care. But if you feel that because you spent money on a date that had you transferring money from savings to checking, a woman is supposed to lay with you, you are sadly mistaken sir. I will cordially invite you to get the fuck out my face. And sis, if you feel obligated to sleep with a man after he spent a few hundred on a date, something is wrong. I'd reconsider dealing with this man and check myself as well. Do all dates have to be expensive? NO! Absolutely not! Again, it's about the experience and the quality of the date not the cost! We can do a million things outside of bussin up money in a swanky restaurant. There are tons of great places to eat that don't break the bank! Look, I love a good burger and a mean taco. I love live music and comedy shows. Weather permitting, we can go to the pier, walk around, talk. I absolutely love picnics! Hell, I'd even fry the chicken, cut up the sandwiches, *and* bring the clean blankets and you can bring the drinks and the music, and we can chill *if I like you like that*. Women do not NEED you to take them on expensive dates, we just don't want to hear you complaining that's what we choose to do! So sure we can go have breakfast somewhere, even brunch. We are just dating, right? Regardless, all these things cost. Might not be as much as dinner, but it costs. You are dating a grown woman. It costs to entertain a grown woman. Expenses will be accumulated throughout the date. Even if you don't spend $200 in a restaurant there are other components of the date that's going to cost! Furthermore, there's but so many picnics we're going to go on, bruh. There is no escaping coming out of your pocket when you are dating a grown woman. Because again, *sir*, we can go on brunch dates, that's cool, but you think every time you see a woman you are going to brunch her to death? I don't want another chicken or waffle, *sir.* And no you can't come to my house to chill and I'm not going to yours. So what's up. What are we doin?

Ladies, look, to avoid all of this twerking and conversing with fuck boys who have to carry the damn one every time the bill comes on a date, just date men that enjoy expensive dates as well, to avoid all this tomfoolery about how much a date costs and talks of gold diggers if it means that much to you. All this arguing with somebody's dusty son about feeding you is wack. Lemon pepper wings are cool but not all the damn time. I remember this guy took an interest in me once. After a few conversations he asked could he take me out to dinner. I said yes. He asked me where I would like to go, I said I wasn't sure. He said okay, find a place and let me know. I found a place, I let him know by sending him the link to the restaurant. I didn't hear from him for about 3 days after the fact. He apologized and said that 'his daughter was sick' *negro please.* He then asked me if I wanted to grab a bite to eat after work. I said sure. This fool says to me okay, I know a cool spot by my house with some real good take out. Who did this joker think he was talking to? So you ignored my restaurant suggestion because you didn't want to spend the money or you didn't have it to spend, then you come back with some take out shit? Boy fuck you. And don't have the dusty sons dating you during hoe hours all the time either. Let a man know he gotta take you out while the sun is still shining! You are a grown woman *and* you bad. Don't have nobody hiding you! And if you're out there laying it low and spreading it wide for somebody, and they make you feel as if you can't ask them for anything or they don't treat you nicely by taking you to quality places or spending quality time with you, then there is a huge problem. That doesn't even make sense. Don't date a man who takes issue in spoiling a woman if you like to be spoiled in that way; it's that simple. You can't force him to spend more, and he can't force you to want less, so leave one another alone. Shit, on a good day I'm sure even someone as earthly as India Arie doesn't want no damn shea butter and chill in the backyard for a date. She wants to go out with a man that's going to bust up a few bands! If your bae is beefing about $200 dates, what kind of life do you think you are going to have with this man when it comes to paying bills and living together? How do you think he's going to deal with grown man responsibilities? You think this is the kind of man that will provide for you and gift you with stability and security? You can forget about him being the head of household, just be friends and make him your roommate or be by your self. You are a grown woman, and you are single. You should not be out here bullshittin' with your time if you're looking for a relationship! Now, I don't know if there is a woman reading this right now that's laid up next to some broke cat in a room on 50 thread count sheets with the oven door open to heat up his lil room in his mama's house. You both are sexually frustrated because not only is his bed uncomfortable and hard as shit, but *he can't get hard* because *you can't get wet,* and you can't get wet because you're lowkey turned off and disappointed knowing that you are playing yourself by being with a man that ain't got shit, and he knows that you are lowering your standards for him. The point I'm making is this: he's not going to admit that! He's going to hang on to you for dear life so that you won't recognize your worth. Now just imagine yourself in a King-sized bed, your freshly washed body laying across some deep pocket 1800 thread counts, your King bringing you a glass of wine as you watch TV on his 1000-inch Smart TV screen, cuddled up, sniffing Chanel cologne off his neck, while thinking about the excellent dinner you cooked to perfection in *his* stainless steel pots. *His.* You actually went to the supermarket and bought the groceries because it's nothing to cater to a grown ass man that got it going on. Sex isn't an issue, you're lubricated for the Gods based alone off of the ambience of how he lives and carries himself. That sex hit different when you can spend a night and be comfortable at a man's place, don't it? Date the kind of guy that might be capable of reimbursing you for all those dinners you cooked and groceries you bought as a kind gesture. No, he doesn't have to do that, but the fact that you spent money on him no matter how small, lets him know that you're not stingy, you're not selfish and that you are not waiting around on him to take you out so you guys can eat. But if he doesn't have a kitchen to call his own, I'll go upside your head with a skillet for cooking up gourmet meals for him. Which brings me back to the financially challenged fellow that you're entertaining. How many times have you fed and brought food over and he didn't give you anything in return but back shot mania and promises of *"when I get on I got you"*? Imagine right now that it's the dead of winter, it's cold as hell outside and you can't go to your boo's house because he lives in a cold ass basement, or he doesn't have a (reliable) car to come get you or he doesn't have money on his card to pay for your uber so he tells you to pay for it, *he got you next time*, or even worse his credit is fucked up so he doesn't have a credit card or he has a roommate because his grown ass can't pay bills on his own, or he lives with his mama, or you always have to bring the groceries to his house to cook because he stays in between checks and never wants to take you out because why spend all that money in a restaurant when you guys can just order some processed bullshit from up the street and get a bottle, or he's always trying to pregame before you go out, so he won't have to spend money on drinks in the restaurant, or his hairline always shabby because he can't afford a cut, or you guys can never go on vacation because his money is always fucked up or he just aint never got it, so you either wind up paying for everything or out of guilt you just don't go anywhere. Women want men who got it. What's going to happen if you get in a bind, huh? You can't even call on him, you gotta go behind his back and call Nate because ya mans...*your* mans, ain't got shit! What happens if your direct deposit didn't go through for some reason, so now your check is stalled for 7-10 days. You mean to tell me that you're okay with not being able to call the man you are spending time with because you know he aint got it or even worse, he does, and won't give it to you? Are you out of your mind? Does your mama know you out here dating and crying over broke ni**as? Come on, sis. Now your life is on hold and you're miserable because you lowered your standards to be with someone who doesn't care about the quality of life. You are stuck in a relationship with a man that looks to you to carry the load. Oh but he's nice right? Girl bye.

Now back to what you deserve, imagine your check being stalled but you don't even trip because you know he got it, and you know he will give it to you. *"Babe, guess what, my check is on hold by the bank because I put in the wrong routing number on my direct deposit slip."* Before you even finish your story, he's like, *don't worry I got you so anyway, do you have any vacation days left over? I want to book a trip for us."* You're looking around your office like you're being punked. Yes, it's that easy if you get a man that has his stuff together. Or back to brokey. Come on, sis. Don't let anyone shame you into thinking you are wrong for wanting to date up and date the best! Again, the presence of his finances doesn't mean the absence of your own! You deserve a good life. You deserve to eat good, go on trips, go out on dates, and be treated like the good, hardworking, grown woman you are. If that makes you a gold digger, well shit then, I got a spare shovel in my closet if you need it! Better to be a *so-called gold digger* instead of messing with some broke ni**a. Damn that. You will never be able to enjoy a quality life with a man that doesn't have his finances in order. It's not about depending on a man to do for you; it's about a grown man not being on his job and a woman making smart decisions. Don't play yourself. The same one trying to convince you to settle wouldn't give this same advice to his daughter now, would he? If you don't pay your rent, you will get evicted. If you don't pay Con Ed, your lights will get cut off. If you don't cook, you won't eat. If he doesn't pay the pussy bill, then he can't chill. He can't show up to the dice game without bank so why are you allowing him to show up to you without bank? Women respect men that got it and that gets to the bag! And men respect women who *recognize* and *respect* the men who get to the bag. Don't let that go over your head.

The moral of the story is this:

Look an enword dead in the eyes and ask him this; What's the procedure when there's a grown woman in your face?

8 NOT GON CRY

I'm assuming that if you want to be a wife, a life partner to somebody, or you truly want real meaningful love, then it will do you no good running around here acting like you're a savage. Dope line by Rihanna and all, if you are indeed a savage, rejoice! But if you know that deep down in your heart you want love, then why be a hard rock when you really are a gem? You are going to wind up twerking for the wrong enword pretending to be something you are not. This attitude and behavior are the result of letting folk's dusty son aggravate your nerves for too long. If you are not a savage then pretending to be a savage will attract the wildest animals in the jungle, sis. Oh you think the dusty son got you mad as hell, wait until you start running with the real animals all for the sake of being a savage. You are not about that life, *trust me.* When you claim yourself as a savage, the hyenas will come out to play, baby! The Lions and Tigers and Bears will hunt you down and treat you like the savage you claim to be. And once you get caught up in that mentality it takes a moment to come from under all those bodies trying to lay on top of you. Every day of your "savage" living life you will spend getting back shots and ignored calls from men because they are going to feel as if you don't care about men. You're a savage, right? Bitches get fucked and dissed everyday B. You won't be treated nicely. You will be treated like a savage hoe, henny shots at the bar, back shots in the car. No holding hands, no kisses, no good morning texts, no how was your day, no care bear stares, no soy sauce, nothing. Just random "Wyd" texts at 11 at night when all you really want is a, *"I miss you, when can I see you again?"* text from a man who truly respects and values you. And baby girl that is what you deserve. You deserve to be loved, respected, adored, and wanted. Everybody wants to be a savage, heartless, on some "fuck love" shit. It's not cool. Love is where it's at! At this stage in the game, assuming that those of you reading this are either *a) women of age that are ready to settle down or b) women in general that's simply tired of men not doing right by them,* either way, it doesn't make sense to surround yourself with men who aren't looking for wives or anything long term. If you want something in this life, no matter what it is, you need to surround yourself with the likes of it. Otherwise, you will always feel out of place because you will be. You will be surrounded by a bunch of vultures trying to take from you, and we all know that vultures surround dying things. Are you dying or living? You are not a savage. You are just fed up right now. Being a savage is all fun and games until you wake up to 6 different dick pics, wyd texts, and sexual advances from a bunch of men that don't care about you. It will weigh heavy on you especially if you know in your heart that you really just want a good man in your life. When you hit that level of low, it's going to hurt even worse than the heartache that catapulted you into Thotville. You are going to be mad at yourself for allowing the actions of another to affect your life in such a way. Because while you're out there thottin' and boppin' because of a broken heart, the ni**a that broke your heart ain't even thinking about you. He's already halfway ruining some other woman's life. Resist the urge to go on a dick binge because you feel as if one person couldn't see your worth. Nine times out of ten it wasn't you he deemed unworthy, it was himself. So put the wine down. Turn off that Toni Braxton right now! Don't do it Ms. Celie, don't trade places with where I've been. Don't call him, don't send that long ass paragraph. Don't post the sad ass memes. Don't change your name on social media to "Tasha Fuck Niggas Get Money God First Bitches Can Have Him I Can Do Better Living My Best Life I Aint Going Back and Forth with You Niggas" Johnson. He doesn't care. Breathe. Just Breathe, close your eyes, quiet down on the inside. *Shhhhh*. Hush mama's, find some relaxation.

I know your heart is broken. I know you are just fed up with being a good woman and these bastards out of Carolina don't show you any appreciation. We need to get a petition going for some good woman reparations or something. Yes, we deserve back all the years that the

TWERKIN AND THE CITY

fuck boys took! We will all go through a period in life where we are tired of trying, tired of getting hurt, played, and lied to. We often wonder if being a decent woman is even worth it as we watch the hoes and more free-spirited women *appear* to have more fun than us and seemingly get treated better. But baby, you don't know what anybody else is going through or receiving. You don't know if your friends are happy or fronting in their relationships and marriages, and you don't know if your hoe friends are really living their best lives. All you need to worry about is how *you* feel inside, what *you* want, and what *you* must do. But for now, you must accept that this is the season you're in right now, single and fed up. It's just a season mamas. Take this time to work on yourself as much as possible. Take this time to heal and try new things out because once you start sitting around *over thinking* and *replaying* shit in your head, you are going to find yourself out there in them streets, lonely, desperate, fucking for attention, and doing things that you normally wouldn't do to fill a void. You're going to find yourself on social media posting those wack ass memes for attention and doing all kinds of weird things to get through this. I get it. It's hard sometimes to sit still when you are hurting or wanting. But you can't get sucked into a life that doesn't serve you, and you truly aren't about. That life doesn't deserve a beautiful soul like you. They are not worthy of your presence even if it's only temporary. We can't let the actions of a few bad apples dictate how we move forward. It's about discipline and discernment beloved! Stay true to yourself sis or you will wind up making temporary decisions that may cause permanent damage. Sure I agree, we should all take a break from dating and serious relationships to get into ourselves and have some fun. I believe and am an advocate for a <u>healthy</u> hoe phase because the hoe phase is where you learn yourself. But a phase is just that, *a phase.* There are some real live savages out there, I mean *real* man eaters, *real* gold diggers, *real* hoes, *real* non-give-a-fuckers out there, real ass bitches who don't give a fuck about a ni**a, and even those *bitches* have men that they love and start families with. These rappers sell you a dream about being a thot, hoe, getting money, but they are laid up with newborns and husbands! Don't follow that! Follow your heart! You want love, admit it and be okay with that. Stand in your truth. Ride that frequency sis. Stay in love with the idea of love and don't ever let it go. Don't dumb down how you love and if any man makes you feel as if you need to then sugar, he's probably not the one. Right now you just lost hope in love, so take the time to love on yourself some more, be kinder and more patient with yourself. Because on some real shit, love is so dope. I love being in love. I love being loved, hell, even when it is a lie. It just feels so good. I don't care how many times I get hurt, I'll never give up on love, and you shouldn't either. And not to say that you don't love yourself enough now, but you can never love yourself enough, so find things to do to occupy your head space, get busy living. You don't want to be a savage and miss out on a good man by treating a decent guy like crap just because you had a string of bad relationships and situationships. It's hard not to act up, I know. Listen, between me and you, I got an enword right now I want to lay my hands on, but I'm a woman of prayer, so I chill. But do you know how many times I've prayed to God, talked to him about the anger that was brewing in my chest like, *Lord, listen, I know what you said about vengeance being yours and all that, but dammit can you let me get a few licks in my G and I'll repent immediately after?* But we got to *woosah* and chill. We just must. We can't give nobody that much dominion over us and our actions. We must learn how to heal, grieve, and make room for better things. We must stop breaking our own hearts by expecting more from someone who we know will never change. You're not a savage, you are just having a savage moment. Let it pass, don't let it consume you. If you run out there doing hood rat things with your friends, and you know you aren't about that life, you are going to feel even worse when you're done playing yourself. Sometimes you got to just sit in your stuff and own it. Because despite what you want to believe, you played a part somehow in your heart being broken. I know you don't want to hear this but whether you ignored red flags, dated someone forbidden, kept forgiving and allowing disrespect, or didn't listen, you contributed in some way to the fuckery. And at some point, you allowed the same thing to happen repeatedly either by the same person or different situations. Insanity is what they call it. Now you're mad, wanting to fight and fuck everybody. That is not the solution baby doll. Sit still and let it burn, let it hurt, cry, cuss, scream, and let it out. Then you have to breathe, inhale, exhale, train your mind and heart to think positively, to heal, and to pump again because nobody is going to come and save you. Nobody is going to heal you, only you can do that and when you do, you can't allow the same behaviors that you once did. I say this time and time again, never go food shopping when you are hungry, you will wind up buying a bunch of things you don't need. Same with men, don't go out there looking when you are hungry. You are going to wind up dealing with a lot of bullshit you don't need. You can't go back to the place of hurt for healing or think that things will be different this time. You must move on from that space and time totally. Say it with me, *"I am not a savage, I'm a beautiful flower and I deserve to be watered daily, nurtured, fed, loved, and taken care of delicately."* Continue to bloom, sis. It's time to stop giving our bodies to men that we are ashamed of, and we can't brag about, we aren't proud of, and we simply settled for during our savage moment. Men we met in purgatory, men we know don't mean us any good, men that don't have us on their radar for the future, men who don't ride or die for us and have our backs, men who don't build us up and want better for us, men who don't represent us and uplift us. Because guess what, while you are settling for him? He is also settling for you. There is nothing worse than being with someone who is settling for you. He feels shitty and so he will make shitty decisions. And guess who he considers a shitty decision. You! And why? Because you are out here settling too. You see how that shit works and will eventually backfire on everybody? We gotta stop kidding ourselves and wasting time with men who we know in our hearts won't be around in the next few months. We must practice patience while protecting our peace. We can't be so quick to want to lay up under another to get over the previous brother. We must stop twerking for the wrong enword and absorbing the energy of these toxic men. We have to practice self-control and really and truly want better for ourselves. We have to stop settling for the good and go for the great. There is greater out there no matter how good you thought the last man was because if he was all that good, he would be there. Go for the great sis because you are the great! You must teach these men how to treat you by how you treat yourself! We got to stop wasting so much time correcting a mistake because we don't want to hear *I told you so.*

We must own our shit, dust our shoulders off, and keep it moving. There is so much courage and growth in owning your mistakes and pushing past it. It's so beautiful on the other side. We must stop wasting time, ladies. We must stop being forced and guilted into *"being a man's peace and his ride or die"* without getting the same treatment and respect from him in return. Instead we must start saying *fuck that and fuck you, I can't want better for you than what you want for yourself!* We must know we are worthy of and quite capable of being with a **fully assembled man** who isn't looking for a mother but a woman, a life partner, maybe a wife, but most definitely a best friend. Give yourself the world sis and leave no stones behind for anyone to throw at you. Take time between these heartaches, clear your mind, accept what you just experienced, acknowledge what you just went through, be honest with yourself about it, and then heal, baby. Now I'm no psychic but something tells me that the future is bright for you, and you won't get the love you deserve if you are out here acting an ass based off of what some fuck boy did to you. You got more loving to give *and get!* Love on yourself, cry, scream, write it down, eat it away, drink it away, just don't give it away ever again to the one that threw it away in the first place.

The moral of the story is this:

You are not a result of what happened to you. You are beauty for ashes.

Message!

Women remain broken hearted for too long. Meanwhile men will pick up move on start a whole new life and make you question if what you had with him was even real. We remain hurt over one dude forever, watching the wheels of the bus go round and round, singing Adele's Hello, getting fat off of wine and shit. Just an observation. Man listen, I'm not rushing your healing sis, I've been there. But get your ass up and out and go LIVE!

9 THE GHOST OF FUCK BOY PAST

So there's a new method of bitchassness going on, in which some of you probably have experienced. It's when a guy pursues you relentlessly, wines and dines you, sometimes for weeks, maybe even months. You begin liking him, he's awesome, you tell your girls all about him. You guys even cross the line and get intimate, it's all good and then one day he doesn't call you. You assume he's probably busy, no big deal. You sent a text, *hey baby you good today?* No answer, you raise a brow, but shit happens, so you don't sweat it. The next morning you wake up, no response, you go to work with him on your mind wondering if he's okay, so you text again, *busy?* No response, WTF. By day 3 you're thinking he must be dead or in jail. You read old text threads making sure you didn't say something to turn him off. You remember the last time you were with him, it was nice, fun, you guys got along great. 7 days go by, he texts, *"hey sorry my bad was caught up with work, etc."* You respond with something bland like *glad you're okay, want to meet up for dinner this week?* You do miss him, and you want to ask him to his face, *where the f** you been for real for real,* but you keep it cute on the phone because you want to bait him. But your day in court will never come as he hits you with the, *"I'll see, I'll let you know."*

He never lets you know.

You never hear from him again. You've officially been ghosted.

> *Throws a full plate of food against the wall** Why do men do that?

This is what we are up against ladies. Getting to know a man, even being a "good girl" and making him wait. Being cautious, spending time, doing things the right way. We loosen up and have fun then the moment we catch feelings, a fuck boy earns his wings and flies out of your life. The sad thing is that we can't stop ghosting from happening. There is no build up or signs that it will happen and who is going to be the one to do it. One day you're throwing back shots of tequila and cruising down the west side highway thinking he might be the one, the next you're being ignored and left on read. Then men wonder why we choose to remain single for long periods. It has turned into a game of let's see who dumps who first. Being ghosted leaves a woman with a feeling of shame and inadequacy that later turns into anger and resentment. It makes us afraid to step out and meet someone new. Dating is an energy drainer as is, as well as being a time consumer. You spend so much time getting your outfits right, your hair done, nails, make-up, and babysitters. You make time to meet someone new and entertain them. It takes time to warm up to a stranger and the moment you do, bam he's gone with the wind, no rhyme or reason. I mean so what do we do when someone ghosts us? Sadly there isn't anything that we can do. Most times when a man ghosts you, he doubles back some time later, with some lame excuse about how life was kicking his ass, or he had "a lot going on." At this moment in time, I hope you have found a new boo, or that you are strong enough to not give him the opportunity to play you again. I can't imagine what excuse a man can give you to make you take him back after abruptly exiting your life and breaking your heart. And I am not sure where you would have to be in your life to allow this unstable creature to crawl back into your world. This isn't a "self-esteem" issue because all the bad decisions that women make don't point back to having low self-esteem. Many times we do love ourselves, we see the good in people, we give the benefit of the doubt, and second chances. It's not because I didn't love myself enough, and so I let him do this to me—whatever "this" may be. Sometimes we are just plain ole stupid. Sometimes we settle because we don't have any fight left in us because relationships are draining as hell when they aren't right. Sometimes we just want something for a little while, to fill a void. We need sex, we need some testosterone around us because we are at work all day with women and we talk to our girls all day, so we let in anything with dick and balls just to fill a void. But you got to be careful because you never know who you will fall in love with. When that Jones is coming down there is nothing you can do to stop it. And if you're spending your free time with a fuck boy, and you find yourself in love, welp! It's pimp or die.

You find yourself confused. You don't understand why a grown person is acting this way. You start creating scenarios in your mind about what it may possibly be. Let me assure you of what it ain't. He didn't fall back because he's a Sagittarius and Sagittarius men need to be free, and as a woman you have to give him space to come around so that he can say how he feels, because the sun is rising in his Leo moon and the sun hasn't set in his fire sign of Pisces at 10:04am on a Tuesday morning, plus we are in Mercury Retrograde so give him a few weeks before he reaches out, because his zodiac sign be bugging, especially when Mercury is in Micro Braids. It's not because he's probably not used to a woman like you. It's not because he's probably scared. It's not because things are moving too fast. It's not because he wants you to chase him a little bit. STOP IT! Men do not play hard to get, he's just not that into you! He's not *on you* sis because he doesn't want you! Own it! Deal with it! It doesn't make you less of a woman because he doesn't want to be with you. It doesn't make him a bad person because he acted on his decision. What makes him a bad person is his intentions from the gate and how he handles things. But he is entitled to not like you anymore. You've had men you didn't like any more, right? How did you handle it? Did you consider his feelings? All I know is that it is not your job to stress this enword into wanting to be with you. Don't let your pride or ego have you chasing this enword down because you feel rejected! Let the child support unit chase his ass. Don't be out here begging and chasing nobody's dusty son for answers! You don't need anyone to spoon feed you your worth. Consider the fact that he wasn't good enough for you and he realized it, so he bounced! Stop taking everything to heart! Everything is not a personal attack on you. Yeah, it hurts, it stings, it sucks, but we must keep it moving and not spend so much time romanticizing *one guy*. There are other fish in the sea! There's another man out there with more inches, more bank, and a better tongue game, so go on out there and let him be lead to you by your light! They are out there! I know you want to be boo'd up. But you have been single all of this time and you have been through so much. Don't let it all be in vain. Wait! He's coming sis, I promise you. He has to come sooner or later. God is not going to have you out here lonely for much longer, he makes somebody for everybody! Right now he is preparing the perfect one for you, but how can he catch up with you if you're busy chasing someone that's running from you? Don't let being alone have you ignoring the shortcomings and the red flags of fuck boys. Don't give another dusty son a pair of wings by making excuses for him! If a man wants you nothing will stop him from getting you, it's that simple. Men seek, hunt, pounce on, kill, bag and tag you when they want you. Game over, you are now off the market. No games to be played, no confusion. You are his, he is yours and he will make sure that you know, feel and understand that. The End. There will be no pause, breaks, wondering or waiting. There will be no confusion. Your confusion is your answer. Move on.

But the Ghost came back with a gang of excuses. Let me stop you right here for this PSA. Ghosting is wack! But more so than that, it's flat out criminal. Imagine somebody stealing a car but they don't tell you. But they come and pick you up and take you for the ride of your life in it. Suddenly they jump out of the car while it's still moving. You have no idea what's happening but all you know is that you have to grab the wheel and stop this car from crashing. You can't even worry about the other person until you gain control of the vehicle. Once you pull over you realize that person brought you out into the middle of nowhere just to abandon you and you are left to find your way back home alone. That's ghosting my ni**a! The dusty sons come into your life, most times with an agenda, then leave without a trace of their ashy ass whereabouts. They stop calling, they block you, they send you to voicemail. It's terrible, it's disrespectful, its cowardly, it's hurtful and it's unnecessary. But here you go, taking your Casper back. You're open off of his words and not his actions. He says sorry. He gives you some cockamamie excuse as to why he left you in the middle of the Van Wyck with the engine running. You're thinking see, I knew I wasn't wrong for taking him back. Every chance you get, you let your girls know that he's at your house. Your friends can't even call and ask you how your day was without you responding, *"My day is fine, me and Brian was here all day chillin."* Nobody asked you about Brian! But you have something to prove. Your insecurities about what folks think of Brian has you giving him more honorable mention than he deserves. That's a problem sis, a really big problem that what your folks think of your boo matters to you. That's because you know he ain't shit. But you're in love now, or in deep like, but either way your feelings have intensified in one way or another. You and the Ghost are doing your thing, then one day you call him, and his phone is going straight to voicemail. You're sick to your stomach, panicking. *Please don't let him pull this shit again!* Even being with a man that is capable of ghosting on you is too much to deal with. He's unreliable, untrustworthy, but you gave him wings when you forgave him now he's acting all fly. Fuck boys only earn wings when we don't reprimand them and make them pay for their disrespect. The ghosting has begun again. He calls you two days later with some bullshit excuse, he swings by to keep you calm, and then after that, he ghosts you again. Now you can't even lean on your girls because you stunted on them with this magician, and you don't want to hear the chorus of "mmm hmm and I told you so's." It's not worth it, sis. You need a man that walks the walk and talks the talk. A man that shows up and shows out for you. The first time a man shows you that you can't depend on him, you better believe him sis! Or he will have your ass out here looking hella crazy! Once a ghoster, always a ghoster. When he leaves, let him stay gone. Or the next time he leaves he's going to take your edges with him because you fittna be stressed the hell out chasing him. But while you're chasing him, keep in mind that you only have to chase what's running from you.

The Moral of The Story Is This:

Sometimes you have to treat people how your grandma treated you in the summertime when you were little. Won't be no running in and out of here.

Next time you leave out, stay out!

10 BIG DICK ENERGY

Make no mistake about it. Sex is indeed a weapon. At some time or another we all used what we had to get what we wanted. But there are some men out here with some powerful rods. You can see them coming a mile away. They give off what women like to call, "Big Dick Energy." Big Dick Energy hereafter referred to as BDE is real ladies, don't you get suspicious! I'm here to tell you, that if you are not secure in your sexuality, and if you are not experienced even as a grown woman, it is in your best interest to steer clear of BDE having enwords. They specialize in tearing down walls and confusing the fuck out of women. I know you're wondering, how can I tell if a man has BDE? Listen, he can be 4ft 11. Short men has never been your thing. But you better believe if he has BDE, you will make an exception for him. BDE has nothing to do with money, height, or complexion. Listen, BDE doesn't even mean that he has a big dick either. I know, I know right?! Listen. BDE is serious and once you encounter a man with BDE you won't have a say so in him ruining your life for a good 8-10 weeks. He will have you digging in your bra like "Big Mama" offering him money, whipping up fish and grits for breakfast. Listen, it's real. I've seen it happen.

But see here's the thing about (some) men with BDE. They know that they have something that most women want. BDE comes with swag, charm, gorgeous smiles, good personalities, and they know how to show a woman a great time outside of the bedroom as well. They lure you in with all that silky talk, then BAM you wake up the next day crying, and you don't know why. Next thing you know he's saved in your phone as "King" and he don't even fuck with you like that, but he done ruled your pussy and now you are delusional, dickmatized, and chasing behind this man in the daytime with a flashlight and a mattress tied to your back. BDE had your knees by your ears, tears rolling down your face while he's looking down at you like roadkill, all the while you're thinking about how much you love him. But you really don't. The BDE makes you feel that way. They frazzle your nerves and have you smoking cigarettes at night. BDE has you stalking his social media and texting him in the wee hours of the morning with smiley faces and hearts after each text. BDE takes a nap in your bed when he is done mollywhoppin your insides, and you don't even lay next to him. You go sit on your couch, staring at your bedroom door wondering what in the hell just happened in there. What happened in there was a homicide. A murder if you will of all your good common sense. You don't even care no more about how you look in front of this man. You're whipped! Just put yellow tape around your bed and call it a day. Listen sis. Get yours. Do you. But even the strongest of women have flipped the script and lost their cool over some BDE. BDE will have you pairing his socks and ironing his work clothes for the week and he ain't even got no job. BDE will have you sleeping with him at his mama house in that same twin bed he grew up sleeping in. BDE will have you crying during sex for no reason because BDE makes you put your guards down and relinquish control of everything, why, because sex connects people as is...and we cannot pretend that it means nothing. You are exchanging bodily fluids with someone else. You're being intimate, kissing, loving, sucking, enjoying one another's flesh, consistently. There is no way that you will not catch feelings; and when you catch a soul tie with a BDE, it makes it even worse. Sex can be good, but if you are dealing with a man that has BDE, you will become insatiable. You find yourself wanting to do everything for this man and he's not yours. He doesn't desire you in the way that you desire him. He's well within his rights to tell someone *"It ain't like that with us"* when they ask what's up with yawl. Oh girl and when you hear that, you lose your fucking mind! You feel as if he disrespected you. But no, it is you who decided to play lieutenant in this man's life without his permission or need for you to do so, because BDE got you twisted out of your mind thinking it's one way but it's the other way. Because when BDE makes love to you, he treats you like you are his wife in bed. He makes you feel as if you are the only one, the best one. He takes his time and concentrates on every part of your body, even your mind...*especially your mind.* He's never going to stop you from catering to him, pleasing him, and being all over him. Listen, these enwords will turn into a whole pumpkin on your ass at midnight, fuck around. One minute you got a whole sexy ass BDE having man in your face, the next minute he done spun into gold dust like Michael Jackson in Remember the Time. Got you looking around the bedroom like I know he was just here! This is what his energy does to many women not just you. And to be frank and crass at the same damn time, yes sometimes the dick be so damn delicious you happily play the fool. Between the dick, the swag, the smell, the smile, just everything all wrapped up in one, man just shove a stick up my ass and call me a candy apple! But once his roster gets too full, oh, your ass is going somewhere! Someone is going to have to get let go and if it's you, my condolences. Now you're sick to your stomach but Effie we all have pain! The loss of an Alpha Male with BDE is known to be one of the top 10 causes of edge loss in women across America. It's a real sucker punch to the gut. The Real Big Booty Judy drops can't help you, and Wild Growth isn't going to help. You are going to have to purify yourself in the waters of Lake Minnetonka, sage, burn Frankincense and Myrrh, fast for 40 days and 40 nights, block him, delete the thread, change your name, and move out of the country before you even begin to sprout edges again.

In all seriousness, it's nice if you can lock down a BDE, and he commits because eventually they do settle down. If he's yours, then by all means take your BDE down to Old Town Road and ride him until you can't no more. But if you know that you are looking for more and he isn't, I'd avoid all BDEs especially if you are a woman of age. I know it's hard when you're 40+ and single because we are in our prime and ready to pounce on everything! Women in their 40's want sex all day. But what do you do with that overwhelming feeling of loss and emptiness now that the good times are over? It's now back to square one. Wishing you didn't do it, wishing he had more to offer than his BDE. We must learn and practice self-control at some point in our lives, ladies. Our sanity, self-respect and hearts are at stake. Our bodies deserve better, our minds deserve better. We deserve better than a temporary thing. You deserve your eternal love. A man that is ready to love you. If all you want is fun and games, then, do you!! Just know that messing with BDE is all fun and games until he changes his number and *forgets* to give you the new one.

The Moral of The Story Is This:

Stop breaking your own heart!

11 YOU'VE GOT TO SHOW ME LOVE!

Something weird happens when you find yourself single. Most of the time you are happily single, just going about your life doing what you do, but sometimes the shit hits you out of the blue. Some days, single life is no big deal. Having a man doesn't validate you, and you have a full life, but other days you find yourself like *yo! I don't have a man in my life!* Maybe you were triggered when you had to drag the ladder out of the closet, climb it, and change the bulb again. Maybe your back was hurting really bad, and you wished your boo was home to rub you down, but you don't have one. You went out with the girls last night and those Louboutins did a number on your feet. Where is Jody to ease the pain in your Achilles? It's always a quick moment or phase where you feel out of touch. Well at least that's what happened to me. Never in my life did I ever think that I would get to the point of caring about being single. I've been nonchalant my entire life as it pertains to dating. Men came and went. There was never a shortage or panic. I knew the Universe would send me one before I could miss a beat. But you get older and there are certain needs you have as a woman and you look up one day like, wait, where is my boo? And why isn't the Universe sending them as frequently as she used to? Listen, there are times when you are single, and it's all spa days, self-love, mani, pedi, girl's trip, bottomless mimosas, and twerking on the beach because you are fuck boy free and you go to bed at night knowing somebody's dusty ass son isn't cheating on you. Yes, those are the moments where you feel so free and liberated. Your mind is right, your body is right, your soul is right, and you feel so damn superior, ready, on one! But what about those other times. You know the times that come out of nowhere, just when you think you had it all under control and your coochie jumps for no reason reminding you that she aint been touched in months, sometimes years, but there is nothing you can do about it because you are way past scrolling through your phone to send "hey big head" texts. You are way past digging in that box of blues for some undeserving negro with good dick to knock you off only to leave you feeling empty. Nope, you have restraint now. It's above you now, you want no part of the men in your past or anyone in your present that only wants something casual. But nothing is worse than having a man break your celibacy or virginity, and it doesn't go anywhere.

Life is too short for bad sex and mediocre men. You need somebody that isn't afraid to dive balls deep and hit the bottom of that pussy. You need to be with someone that lifts you higher! Someone to laugh with. You need to be with someone that excites you in ways that you have never felt before, a man that knows how to please a woman, cater to a woman, love on a woman, respect and treat a woman. A man that learns you while he earns you. Yes baby! Heartbreaks and promises, I've had more than my share! You've got to show me love! But where is he? You don't even know where to start looking. I hear that at this point in the game, it's not for you to look because he will find you. But shit, is he blind? Girl, I know that feeling. And so, you have moments where you think your standards are too high, or perhaps you just aren't what men are looking for and you give up the search. Your friends convince you to take your pu**y off desert time and go get some, to stop waiting for Mr. Right and give it to Mr. Right Now! And so you figure, hell I'm a grown woman I have needs, and so you get you some. It was all so simple, but your need for male interaction has you open and now your friends are looking at you like girl what did you do? We said go get some dick; not go get stupid! That longing for attention from a man has you delusional, and it has awakened all your vulnerabilities and thoughts and shit after not being touched in so long. No you are not in love, and he is not in love with you. You just fed him some hungry pussy and he is enjoying all that lonely, good pussy energy that you are giving him. Yes. Just like men have Big Dick Energy, women have good pussy energy. You must always protect your pum pum. You put that good pussy energy on the wrong one it's a wrap! Next thing you know, you're making excuses to your girls about why you're sleeping on this man's air mattress while his kids are asleep on the kitchen counters during *his* weekend. Even worse, you wind up back in bed with your toxic ex for familiarity purposes. A lot of women do that (*I have been guilty of such*) because you don't want to raise your body count, and you don't want to give your inner Adina Howard to just anybody so why not give it to the ain't shit ex, but even that gets tired. So now you are back to square one.

Those sad and single moments often come as a surprise, don't they? Picture it: Brooklyn, 2019. It's a Sunday evening when you're done cleaning the house, showered, and shaved; and you decide to cook a good meal for yourself and have a glass of wine. You are feeling *really good* about yourself. Your cute little grilled shrimp salad came out perfect. The house smells all good with scented oils and the remnants of sage are in the air. Your sheets are clean, and your hair smells divine. Your skin is all dewy because you have been sucka free for a long time, drinking water, and minding your business. Somebody's dusty ass son has not been stressing you out. You're dancing in the mirror and turning from side to side checking yourself out. Your stomach is going down and your edges are full. You wink at your reflection. Then it hits you, right at that moment, wine glass in your hand, beautiful goddess in your reflection, that smile fades. *Just a little.* The house gets deafening quiet, not a creature was stirring not even a mouse in that bitch. It's just you and your thoughts now, thoughts of, why am I single? Why don't I have anyone to share my life and love with? Why isn't there someone I can call to come share this big shrimp salad and a bottle of wine with? All this love and good womanisms I have to offer, and all I can think is, why the fuck Big don't want me?

There is absolutely, positively, nothing wrong with you, my beautiful sister. Look at yourself in the mirror one more time and smile! You are a beautiful soul, and any man would be beyond blessed to have you, but you are so special that not just any man can get at you. I know your phone is dry and now you're turning on yourself, thinking that maybe it's you. Maybe your standards are too high, or you put on too much weight, or your ass isn't big enough, your hair isn't long enough, your skin isn't light enough, you don't make enough money, you're not cool enough, you're not wild enough, or you're not ladylike enough. You look around you and you see all these women in relationships, they look happy, they just might be happy, but you do not know the hell they had to go through or what their journey was, allow them to be great without turning on yourself, it's just not your time beloved! Send that prayer up, *Lord, I see what you do for others, send some my way,* and keep it moving! And then you have women who are in relationships *settling,* that is not what you want either, love! You beat yourself up thinking that maybe if you just do this or that someone will want to date you. Baby girl, that is not the case. Somebody is looking for you just as you are. What's happening to you right now is that you have standards. You're serious about who you spend your time with and what you spend your time doing. You don't have the same wants and needs at 40 that you had at 25 and 30. Accept that things are different now. You can't even fathom settling and doing the things you used to do for the sake of getting or having a man. It's not even a thought. Can you imagine settling the way you once did *before* you knew better? This is why you are still single. So when you do meet someone, he has *one time* to stand you up, one time to text some stupid shit, one time to go missing for a day. Women of a certain age are cutting enwords off before they even get on. We are too seasoned to play hokey pokey with these fools. We are not playing games; and yeah, we might be a little too harsh and strict on our policies but so what, that's because we accepted the bullshit in the past, and we're not accepting it now! This attitude alone is going to slim your chances of meeting a quality man. We are not here for any excuses. Men need to make dates and keep them, keep in touch, remain consistent and present, spell your words out, don't ask us WYD and WYA. We are not having that ICDC college bullshit. We get turned off for the smallest things and guess what, we don't care what men think! However, if you didn't have standards and you chose to settle, there is no doubt in my mind that you would have a variety of assholes to date, a shopping cart full of junk food is all that is. Don't let being single chase you into the arms of a fuck boy. There is power in the tongue. You can curse life with it. You can heal folks with it, you can end relationships with it, or start new ones because of it. That tiny muscle can change lives. If you tell yourself something long enough you will begin to believe it. So don't start telling yourself anything that goes against what your heart truly desires. Don't be vague about what you want either. Talk your shit, sis! When it comes to the matter of love and men, you must be clear about what you want for yourself before you step out into the world asking anything of anyone. If you have no idea what you want out of life or a relationship my suggestion would be to stay single and not even interact with men outside of a platonic level because this is how you get taken advantage of and wind up twerking for the wrong enword. What we want is on our minds every single day. We think about our future 99% of the time. We are all working toward some kind of goal. It is my belief that no matter who we are and what walk of life we come from, we all want one thing, happiness, but sometimes we just don't know how to articulate it. It's in our hearts, but we just don't know how to *feel* it and that's simply because we are not ready. The reason is because the truth about what we want isn't done processing, it's still cooking inside of us, so until that bell goes off to let you know that you're ready, then you won't really know how to show or tell someone what you want. Oh, but when you *are* ready and you *do* know what you want, why beat around the bush? Are you afraid that you will chase a man away by appearing too forward, too strong, or too bossy? I got news for you toots, you won't chase the man *for you* away by being up front. You will only chase away the suckers with the truth! Men with an angle won't fool around with a woman that knows her worth, so all you're doing is weeding off the suckas. Because fuck boys beget fuck shit, and they also have heightened senses. They can sniff a confused woman out a mile away, and they know when a weak woman is talking like she's strong. They can hear your cries for attention and boy when they catch your ass, it's a wrap! So stop being vague about what you want. This is your life. These will be your memories, and your heart is on the line. Your happiness and future are at stake here, no one else's. You must put yourself first and fight for the life and love you want and deserve, and that is not selfish. Without a shadow of a doubt you should have your non-negotiables when it comes to dating, assuming that you are dating with a purpose. If you are looking for something serious and you are done playing reindeer games then, yes ma'am, you better step up to the plate with your scroll, your standards, your contract, your non negotiables, and ever so politely let an enword know how it needs to go down with your actions. There's no bending the rules for nobody, not anymore, not now. You did that already. You settled already, you bullshitted yourself enough already. You've come up hard baby, you been through enough. You held enwords down, you ride-ED and dieED, you cried, you settled, you stayed, and you waited. No more! You cannot allow someone into your life that is not going to upgrade it and change it for the better. You cannot date someone that doesn't have anything to offer. We are not dating because we are lonely, depressed, rebounding, or unsure. We are standing strong in our truths with our heads held high and remaining single until someone worthy comes along that we are **PROUD** to claim. This new man that will come into your life has to be sweeter than your solitude. He can't disrupt your peace. He has to come in offering unlimited joy, peace, blessings, and good vibes.

He gotta show love!

You've worked hard, you graduated college, you have the degrees, and the experience. If someone offers you a job paying $12 per hour and tries to convince you that it's all you are worth and ever going to get, and that you are absolutely crazy to think you deserve more, you will look at them like they were crazy! If you put in the work, you get shit done, you know that you are worth a 6-figure salary, including summer and winter Fridays, would you take that $12 per hour job? No, you would keep searching and keep interviewing until someone recognizes your worth and gives you every motherfucking penny you deserve. You're nobody's sob story. You are nobody's broken bird, you are nobody's pity party. You are a woman, that has experienced so much and now it is time to live and be happy. Don't let nobody overwork you and undervalue you. What good does it do for you to play small so that someone else can feel tall? What good does it do for you to deny yourself what you want and deserve? What good does it do for you to stay quiet on matters that you can benefit from speaking up about? Every time you agree to do something that you know in your heart you truly do not want to do, you are saying no to yourself and giving a fuck boy his wings. Why would you deny yourself anything? You have reserved every right to require what you can reciprocate, so talk your shit sis! You can't continue to suffer in silence, being mistreated, and underrepresented because you don't want to rock the boat or ruffle any feathers.

I want to slide back a bit and talk about non-negotiables. Your non-negotiables are *very important* as they are the things special to you that you absolutely need for your mate to bring into the relationship. They help you weed out what you don't need or want. Do you have any? I'll give you one of mine. Self-Respect. A lot goes under that umbrella. I know that most people think that self-respect is reserved for women only. But any man I am dealing with must respect himself as well. He can't be a male thot, and he can't be for everybody. He has to respect his dick. He must respect his time. He must value himself as a man and live his life as such. He must know his worth. He must be about his business. He must overall exemplify what a man is about (for me) which is hard working, loving, genuine, strong, supportive, consistent, and reliable. He, without a doubt, must be mentally and emotionally healthy. There are no ifs ands or buts about it. He must have his mind right and his heart has to be good. He must be a solid man, solid in his beliefs, his work ethic, his wants, his needs, and himself. He must be a man of his word. I can't deal with no bluffers and bullshit artists. My heart can't take a liar and my patience won't allow me to go back and forth with these enwords. Be a man of your word. Test his ass to make sure he is who he says he is. You should be able to count on your guy hands down. You should feel it in your heart and soul that no matter what, your dude is going to hold you down, show up for you, and do what he said he is going to do. You cannot waste time on faulty men. You just can't. These are characteristics that no man can fake, and it won't take long for a woman to realize that he's frontin'. Once I can confirm that he is not a fraud, then I can focus on my other non-negotiables. But without the ones that I named, nothing else matters, not your money, not your degrees, not your 10 inches. Remember ladies, never forget! You date at the level of your esteem. Be mindful of one thing, the non-negotiables are *your secret*, it's not for him to know about. He doesn't need to know what you will and will not accept or what kind of man you are looking for. Your "list" is for you to quietly check in your mind and decide based on that. Because once you tell a man what you're looking for, they will pretend to be that kind of guy long enough to have your ass cooking brownies from scratch at 3am because he has the munchies and just fucked you so good you done lost your damn mind *and job* because you can't get out of bed in the morning. No ma'am, we are not doing that. Then once you're all nutty, he's calling you a crazy bitch and acting like he's not the reason. Wendy Williams did not escape the wrath of Kevin Hunter and have a whole Hot Flash Summer for us to be out here settling for con artists. So I say, less is more when discussing what you are looking for in a man as well as when it comes to discussing your past, keep the stories at a minimum. There is no need to tell a man *everything* about your past. Nope! Aht aht aht! Keep that to yourself. Don't give him the blueprint on how to manipulate you and hit those triggers because that's all you're doing when you're telling him all the ways you were mistreated. What are you telling him for? He doesn't have the superpowers to heal you because he wasn't even there! What you need to do, before you get into any kind of situations with anybody is practice the 48 Laws of Shutting the Fuck Up. Yes. There is no reason on God's green earth that you should give a play by play to any man about the traumas of your past. I speak from personal experience, when I was younger, I felt that if I told the *new* guy what the old guy did that the new guy would fix it, heal me, treat me better, take pity on me, hurt for me, want to avenge the situation for me, and grieve with me. Nah. That was not the case.

First of all, men don't care about what you went through in your past, not on a deep level. Sure, during conversations and getting to know one another you can touch on some things but just know that all of this information is being stored and the moment you step out of bounds you will be reminded as to, *"Why all of your exes cheated on you, why he left you, and why none of your relationships worked out."* Speaking on childhood traumas and how you were raised is important information to share and take in. You need to know what the hell is going on in the minds of men. But the details of your previous relationships are an unnecessary no no. He doesn't need to know so much. What can he do with this information? He can't help you, he can't fix it, or make the hurt go away. He's not going to feel sorry for you and love you better because of what happened to you in the past. He doesn't need to know about things he wasn't present for. Not everything, sis. Handle your business before even jumping into another situation. Heal yourself, so you won't be out here looking for someone to heal you. Practice the 48 Laws of Shutting the Fu** Up and let the new man see the woman that stands before him, the product of such hurtful experiences, standing tall, strong, confident in her skin, not some woe is me, pick me, weak woman looking for someone to love her through the past. This isn't about pretending to be strong, this is about being whole and standing in your truth before you call yourself wanting to date or settle down. Trust me when I tell you, that soft spot deep inside of you is reserved only for the man that can reach it without a map. That sore spot that every man kicked on and beat down is not to be worn on your sleeve. The right man has to get deep enough into your life to find that spot. As far as any new enwords are concerned, you have been treated like nothing less than a Queen by *all your exes,* but it just didn't work out and you're hoping this time it does, PERIODT.

We're not throwing pity parties and waiting for anybody to save us. You are already great! Just know you are single because you have standards now and because this time around you choose to take your time and do the choosing, not be chosen. It has little to do with nobody wanting you and everything to do with the beautiful deserving woman you have become. You are a grown woman. You have been there and done that. Everything you require from a man at this point you should be able to reciprocate. You are an asset, not a liability. You know what you bring to the table, so you're not willing to whip out your fine China and set it down just anywhere. I want to assure you that men are looking at you and second guessing if they are good enough or man enough to approach you. Don't sleep! Make sure you know, believe, and understand that! So walk with your head up! Find reasons to smile! Pull all those pretty outfits out of your closet and wear them for you! Get out of the house, get out of your head, and give the world your energy and beauty. GO OUTSIDE! Being single doesn't mean isolating yourself or letting yourself go. Go where quality men are and when you find out, email me, and let me know so I can come too! Date and hang out with quality people when you are single, because you never know who you will catch feelings for! You want to fall in love with Jodie who ain't got no job? NO. Then stay away from unproductive, unstable creatures. Go get you a good-good man that looks at you like you were just born. Tina Knowles Lawson crawled so that you could run sis! Don't let the leader of the Beehive down! Scream it loud: YOU'VE GOT TO SHOW ME LOVE!

The Moral of The Story Is This:

Anything that settles stays at the bottom.

12 NEW ATTITUDE TAKING OVER FOR THE 99 AND THE 2000

This book is a love letter to myself, and I wanted to share it with you all. I've made more than enough bad choices. I'm self-taught. I fell on my face in public many times, but I got back up and I kept on going. From early on, my relationships were public due to the disrespect that I endured, and as a young woman, you don't really know how to defend yourself against people calling you dumb or dragging you because of what some man decided to do to you. I never got the chance to "hide" what I was being put through. So instead of continuing to be embarrassed by someone else's actions and the opinions of others, I learned to embrace all my flawed relationships because I was eager to learn myself and men. I took a lot of blows to my character, but it made me who I am. I realized that nobody in this world could judge me because what I learned was that most people hide what they are going through. Everybody wants to appear to be perfect. They will whisper their own failures but will turn around and shout yours! I decided to walk with my head up regardless of what someone did to me or what folks had to say about me. I chose to honor myself no matter where I am in life. I chose to honor myself no matter what I had or didn't have. I chose to honor myself despite those who don't. I honor myself no matter what is going on around me. I honor myself regardless of the mistakes and poor decisions I've made. I chose to honor myself no matter what is happening in my life. I chose to honor myself no matter what that man has, no matter who is so called doing better than me. I chose to honor myself through whatever the weather because I've come to learn that I am worthy of respect and love no matter what!!! I had to teach myself that. I waited a long time for someone outside of me to show me and teach me self-love. It never happened. I realized it was all on me to honor myself no matter what. Always make the decision, as soon as you open your eyes, before your bare feet hit the floor, to honor yourself!

In this book, I'm simply suggesting that we begin to date up and stop settling. I want us to learn the traits of, and therefore, avoid toxic men. I want us to explore more and fall in love with life before we aim to fall in love with a person. Let's learn how to date and how to wait! Let's get to know these men on a deeper level. Don't wait until it's too late to find out what's brewing beneath the surface. Let us not be afraid to ask questions about their upbringing and their triggers. Let's delve a bit deeper into their lives and learn about their family pathology. Let's ask those bold questions about his past relationships and learn his views on matters close to your heart. Let's risk losing him if he doesn't want to provide us with the necessary information we need to move forward comfortably. Let's get bold! Let's date like adults! Let's walk away and say no to situations we know aren't going anywhere. Let's *really* get to know these men, ladies, as a staff, a record label, and a crew! But at the end of the day, we are all going to do whatever makes us happy.

No matter how many books you read and no matter how dope the advice is, a person is not going to change until they are good and ready. Your married friend doesn't have the blueprint on how you can get a husband. Her path is her path. Your happily single friend that's juggling a million men is doing what she has been called to do, that's not your lane. My point is, what's for you is for you and in the meantime, live your life! It's not all about improving yourself to get a man! Amen? This era is, in my opinion, way too obsessed with being in relationships. We are so quick to give someone our all to make them happy before we put that much effort into ourselves. But if you are going to date, and if you are in the neighborhood for real love, then this is what I think.

I think that you should be with someone who you can WIN at life with. I'm not talking about matching Benzes and mink coats. I'm talking about winning, spiritually, mentally, emotionally, financially. I imagine a relationship where I make an already good man, even better.

I bring out the best in him, I make him smile more, I make him stronger, I keep him calm, and he keeps me wild— that sort of thing. I imagine a relationship where my man includes me in all his decisions and has me by his side everywhere he goes because he knows that nobody will have his back like I will. The reason my man will be so secure in this fact is because he is secure in how he treats me and takes care of me as his woman. He's not insecure or worried about anything because he does what he is supposed to do, and he is who he says he is. A man that's a man already. I imagine a relationship where nobody outside of us would try to approach us in a way to disrespect our union because they respect our union. It's strong, it's real, it's built on love, trust, admiration, respect, and honor. I deserve that and you are deserving of that, so why settle? What do you imagine as the ideal relationship? Is he kind? Is he safe? Is he trustworthy? Is he reliable. As the viral meme on IG goes, *"Stay single until you come across someone who adds value into your life."* Stay single until you know what you are bringing to the table as well.

I remember after my last relationship, I was drained, you hear me? I was just over men, period! I was tired of these relationships lasting 3 and 4 years then abruptly ending. I was tired of being swept off my feet just to get dropped on my head without a reason. I was sick and tired of wasting my time on situationships, so I just went cold turkey, celibate, no sex, no phone calls, no flirty texts, absolutely no contact with men, period. I needed a do over. I needed to fix my credit and remove everybody off the list that kept my score low. I had to remove them completely and build my credit from scratch. I had to file for personal bankruptcy. When you build your credit from scratch, you're starting off with nothing. It's a blank report now and you must carefully pick and choose who you deal with this time around because you can't allow anybody to mess up your credit. You are getting a second chance at life, you have got to move differently. Folks will deplete you and leave you bankrupt. It's a different game all together once you decide you are done playing games with your life and yourself and you must start over from the bottom. You begin to spend differently, and in this case, I am talking about spending your time differently. You don't overspend this time around because you know you can't afford to. You don't give anyone over 30% of your time because it will bring your credit score down especially if they can't reciprocate what you put out. You must keep it cute now, sis. Folks aren't allowed to be all up in your space with nothing to offer and nothing good to say. No longer can you have a bunch of minor credit cards laying around for small impulsive shopping days. Tighten up. You know exactly what you want and need. You don't need to shop around because you are waiting for that big ticket item to become available and when it does your credit will be good, and you can get it with no problem. That's how you have to look at your life sometimes, ladies. Treat yourself like A1 credit. It felt good to heal myself of past hurts and just start over fresh. Old ways won't open new doors. I had to change my thinking and my approach toward everything, and it changed my life. Sure, I still have my challenges, but I found peace if nothing else. I found clarity. Anything tied to my old ways of being or thinking removed itself. I didn't have to do anything. I began to evolve so high, I didn't have to do the hard labor of cutting folks off, as they were just released from me. The quality of men interested in me has even changed, and the kind of women friends and conversations I have are different. You move differently when you have a black card in your wallet verses a Capital One prepaid. Everything is just different when you finally get honest with yourself, and you push for change. You can no longer accept calls from that big dick monster who only wants to make you cum and cry. You can no longer entertain these enwords in relationships and even marriages, claiming that "it isn't like that." You can no longer believe these men when they say they just aren't ready for a relationship but want the perks of being in one with you. You can no longer waste time dating someone who doesn't know what he wants. You can't be bothered with men who need raising and fixing. That is not your job; you are not responsible for raising and fixing a grown man. It's above you now. And if that means you have to be alone while everyone around you is getting married, having babies, and meeting new love— then fine, that has nothing to do with what's in store for you and your life! You don't know what their path or prayer was. While you're in the waiting period, the key is to *attach your happiness to something outside of a person.* Live your life and have fun! Fill your days up with quality things to do and people who bring you joy. Nobody says you have to be happy every day, but you damn sure can be solid in your faith and what you deserve and walk in that truth every single day. Say **NO** to struggle love. You do not, under any circumstances, have to put up with somebody's hardships as a way to prove your loyalty and worth. Don't listen to these jokers out here trying to convince you that you have to struggle with them before you see the prize. Get the fuck outta here. It is absolutely okay to walk away from and not even take the phone number of someone who does not have their shit together in a way that is conducive to your happiness and what you are looking for. You don't owe anybody your blood, sweat, or tears. You are not less of a woman because you want to bypass a man with potential for someone who has halfway reached their goal already. That potential shit is cool when you're a young woman in your 20's and everybody is trying to figure life out. It's not cool as a grown, seasoned auntie. No ma'am. Shittin' me! Ain't nothing behind potential but a promise and promises ain't nothing but comfort to a fool. You are grown now, you don't have time for practice! Potential ain't nothing but practice! Say it with me: Yes, I do want and *deserve* a finished product. You damn right. And when you finally do attract your King, as I know you will, keep in mind that he should be your biggest cheerleader, and a positive motivating force within your life—you heard Pastor Ron Isley! He should know how to communicate and be comfortable enough to show emotion in front of you. He should trust you. He should need you and want you. He should support you and adore you, he should love on you, and make you feel like the most beautiful girl in the world. He should inspire you by how he lives his life. He should be a leader. He should be your best friend and your confidant. He should motivate you and pray with you. He should be open to learning how to take out your sew-ins. He should hold you tight at night and kiss your forehead in the morning. He should thank God for you. He should never disrespect you, not even at the height of the most intense disagreements between the two of you. He should communicate with you daily and protect your reputation. He should be loyal, faithful, and generous. He should be healed of past traumas and ready and open to receive and give love 100% with no doubt in his mind and when he is, he should come find you because you are so deserving of non-toxic, fresh, real, heaven-sent love from a good, hard working, kind, and loving man. You should smile at the thought of him and cum just from him touching your face. His chest should be the safest place on earth to you. He is reliable, dependable, honored, and respected by his friends and family. Your man should be your teammate, and you should be his. You should no doubt have his back, and he should have yours. You should be so turned on by how well your man does his man thing, because even the hardest most independent Alpha Females, will melt down and become caring, kind, gentle, and submissive to a man if he provides her with the proof of being able to take care of her heart, body, soul, and mind. So what you are a soldier and can hold shit down. That doesn't mean you should accept some man always trying to start a war with you. A man should come into your life and make it easier, calmer, more gentle, sweeter. He shouldn't be bringing hell, worry, stress, grief, financial issues into your life. Being a woman is not easy. We go through things. We have our bad days, we have our insecurities, we have those moments of uncertainty. Your man should be your rock during those times. You should be able to lean on him in your time of weakness. No he will not be perfect, but he will be a man's man and he will have your back. Yes, he will have some issues, but his good has to outweigh his bad and at the very least he should be ready, willing, and able to accept you as partner, accept your help, and be willing to grow and heal with you. He cannot be a *this is who I am, kind of ni**a*. That's not going to work. It's about growth, constantly. Without a shadow of a doubt you need to feel you can trust him. And if you do not feel that way, then you just might be twerkin for the wrong enword. Lil' Kim did not *yeah, what-what* all through the 90s for you to be out here letting fuck boys that don't even have a Primary Care Physician ruin your beautiful spirit and break your heart.

We also must be very clear and open to the possibility that a lot of men don't really like women. They like having sex with us. They like our company. But *they don't really like us.* They pit us against one another, they dispose of us so quickly, they are on to the next like it's nothing, not because they are some kind of cold-hearted don, but because they don't like women, they don't even like themselves, so they will always find something wrong with us, as well as displaying behavior and traits that aren't in our favor. You might have to talk to his mama about that or see how he was raised. Perhaps his ex-girlfriend(s) can give you some insight on him if you care that much. Whatever the case, this sounds like a *"him"* problem. It is your job to peep game in the beginning and run far away from his ass if you get this kind of vibe from him. Go where the good men are! Go where the love is!

Some of you are with men that you know in your heart of hearts you are not being truthful with, because you aren't showing him the real you out of fear of him not liking *the real you*? Why? What the fuck is that all about? You do know that this has more to do with *you* not liking the real you than it has to do with him not liking the real you, right? He doesn't even know who she is! Why do you choose to hide parts of yourself from him? Are you ashamed of it? Do you wish that it didn't exist? Well news flash toots, it does exist, it is a part of you, it is you and it will show up when you least expect it! So if you're out here frontin for an enword and you don't feel comfortable enough around him to be yourself, then guess what, clearly, he is not the one! Put your drawls on and go home!

Some of you are laid up with a man that doesn't sexually satisfy you, for reasons I can't even begin to imagine outside of the fact that he got that bag. But you want more. Money can't fix your sexual cravings. He's not hitting it right. You're constantly thinking about a past lover or a new one that you have yet to find. Your bedroom game is on one hundred. You do all things and everything through dick which strengthens you. But the man that you are entertaining thinks that you are doing too much. He sometimes says things that makes you feel uncomfortable with your sexuality. But this is who you are, you like whips and chains, you like to role play and crawl across King size beds with a bunny rabbit tail attached to your ass. You can fuck all night, you can go! You like to put on ski masks and creep through your man's window to steal the dick sometimes. Oh, it's just me? *Whatever.* But what do you do with that insatiable, sexual appetite of yours? Do you lay up totally unsatisfied because the new boo can't hang? Do you hide that side of you because you feel as if he will judge you? Because I don't know about you, but sexual compatibility and chemistry is at the top of my list when it comes to my needs in a relationship. If I cannot give my entire body to you and be 100% free to be who I am in bed with you, we might have a problem. We may have to have a conversation about why you feel a way about how I perform in bed. I would be curious to know what is on a man's mind that turns him off from a 'sexually free' woman. It's worth having a conversation with your boo just to see where he is coming from and maybe you guys can come to some sort of understanding. He may be interpreting your sexual freedom wrong, he might be insecure, either way, have a conversation and then decide from there. *That's my mature advice.* But what I really want to say is, you tell that limp biscuit, cum when I come or cum when I get back, because

I'm out! Who the hell got time for wack sex? See this is why you must be firm in your non negotiables for yourself as well as for these men. If sex is in your top 5 dead or alive then make sure you get that in your relationship! The dusty son's aren't sitting around being faithful to you, because you're a good girl but your sex is wack. Are you dumb? They are moving on! You only have one life. Are you going to spend it sexually frustrated on top of everything else? Then what's going to happen is, he's going to start making it seem as if you're the problem why his dick won't stand up. *You're the problem.* It's your fault why you're not wet. No sir, the gag is pussy is always wet, and if it's not, that's because the woman isn't feeling you bro! Girl, put some drawls over that dry pussy and go home. Ain't nobody got time for this.

It's time to create beautiful memories! Make room for the good memories by letting go of the bitter-sweet ones. You don't need them anymore. Fuck struggle love, fuck excuses, fuck drama, fuck woe is me, fuck the past, fuck the pain, fuck getting fucked with no love, no respect, no desire to treat you like a goddess. We're not waiting on anybody to love us the right way anymore. We're not chasing and wasting time. We are no longer sending long paragraphs and allowing anyone to come to us "as a woman." Go suck yu muma! We're not waiting anymore. We want what we want NOW! Go to the gym, feel good about yourself, hang out with your friends, spend time alone and love it! Shop, meditate, sleep! Focus on your business and your job! Get Money! All this malarky over these enwords that ain't offering up shit. If he wants your time, then let him prove it! In the meantime, get money! Get better, get flyer, get healthier, get smarter, get doper, get finer! And if that intimidates men, fuck 'em, not your problem. Make up your mind today that you are going to clean up your credit and stop overspending time and resources on people that aren't in alignment with who you wish to become, have already become, and trying to attract. Say it louder for the people in the cheap seats: IT

DOESN'T MATTER WHAT I ACCEPTED IN THE PAST, I'M NOT HAVING THAT

SHIT NOW! Forget the past, forget what you've done and accepted, forget what people are trying to throw in your face, and forget those low standards that you used to have and the folks who are trying to keep you there because your growth means that they will not be able to reach you. Don't let folks carry you like you're some kind of lame. Get feisty, get brand new, glow up, sis! Put yourself first, stunt, you have been humble long enough! You are not stuck up or high maintenance you just know your worth and you know all about selfcare and self-preservation now, because when it's all said and done, when we can't take care of ourselves because we are depressed, sick, and just unable after letting life beat us down and people drag us for filth, that job will replace us, that man will remarry, and friends will move on right after the candle light vigil. Only our babies will be left to fend for themselves and forever grieve the woman who was supposed to be their heroes. We are not the products of our environments or circumstances. We will break generational curses. We are not our mothers, and we are not our fathers. We are better than what we sometimes accept and dish out to people. We are not savages and hoes. We are all works in progress, trying to attain one common goal— happiness. Relationships of all kinds take up our day to day, we are constantly dealing with people be it professional or personal. They push and pull at us all day. It is on us to decide who we keep and who we let go of just as others may choose to keep or let go of us for whatever reason. We must just accept that. In the words of the great Nipsey Hussle, "We cannot possess people, we can only experience them." Unfortunately, we have to keep in mind that nobody belongs to us, and they will not be with us forever, no matter the way in which they are removed from our lives. But it doesn't have to be painful. It doesn't have to end in tears and pain. No more fuck boys, no more toxic men, no more heartbreak and bullshit relationships. No more letting the dusty sons of the world waste your time!

I want every woman to feel loved and to know that she is special no matter what anyone tries to force her to believe. Fuck being obsessed with some dude. You need to be obsessed with yourself! And just know that you can't rush love, you can't do anything but live your best life, and love on yourself *hard* until he shows up! You are here on this earth for a reason, and it is not to be mistreated or disrespected but to give love and receive love. I want us to not waste too much time on the things that have hurt and disrespected us and push forward and get ahead of the pain and heartache and continue striving to be the best people that we can be. So, go where the love is, go where you can grow, go where you are celebrated not just simply tolerated and never ever give up on yourself. Don't pity yourself, don't sit in the dark, don't build up a wall waiting for someone to show you how much they care. Don't give up on yourself and don't stop living. Get your beautiful self-up and keep going! Pour into yourself and fight for the life you want and deserve. No matter how hard life is you are here, which means you have another shot at getting things right. Listen, folks are going to disappoint you for the rest of your life. And I know folks like to say no expectations, no disappointments, but to me that is not realistic. When you care about people, and you believe that they care about you, you do expect them to act accordingly. Why else would you bring someone into your world if you expected them to hurt you or disappoint you? Sis, look. At this stage in the game, if you aren't disgusted with some of the things that you have accepted and some of the enwords you dealt with, then you have some more growing to do. If you want more then stop settling for less. If he makes you cry more than he makes you smile, if he makes you feel insecure, if you don't feel safe with him, if you're not growing with him, if he isn't teaching you shit, if he's not loving, if he doesn't make you a priority, if he hates on you, if he isn't supportive of you, if he's not your ride or die, if your soul doesn't feel protected when you are with him, if he doesn't make you straighten your back a little and want to be better than you already are, if life gets worse, more burdensome once he comes around, get rid of his ashy ass. Don't you lose not one summer fucking around with somebody's dusty ass son! And the key to keeping your head up and staying fly through all this shit is loving yourself harder than they hurt you. For each heart break, love yourself harder; for each letdown, love yourself harder; for each betrayal, love yourself harder!!!!! Don't let another dusty son fuck up your PH balance. You can have it all. You deserve it all. You know you do. Don't let people tell you that you can't have it all! Knock down and run over any motherfucka who tries to convince you otherwise. Fuck with who fucks with you. Because twerking for the wrong enword has more to do with what *you* accept than it has to do with what *he* has to offer.

I love you.

Purpose Publishing est 77

Don't miss out!

Visit the website below and you can sign up to receive emails whenever Ayana Ellis publishes a new book. There's no charge and no obligation.

https://books2read.com/r/B-A-CFUEB-GMNAD

BOOKS 2 READ

Connecting independent readers to independent writers.

About the Author

Brooklyn native Ayana Ellis has released 9 books, 7 independently, beginning in 2007 starting with a short story titled, Last Woman Standing which can be found in Girls From The Hood Part 4 released under Urban Books. Her other titles include, Love Changes, Full Circle, King Me, King and I, Don't Be A Dumb Bitch, The Book of Yaya 12:77, Twerkin And the City and Daughters, which is part 1 of a trilogy to be released May 2024.